MEMOIRS OF A
GOOD-FOR-NOTHING

JOSEPH von EICHENDORFF

MEMOIRS OF A
GOOD-FOR-NOTHING

Translated by
BAYARD QUINCY MORGAN

FREDERICK UNGAR PUBLISHING CO.
NEW YORK

Translated from the German
AUS DEM LEBEN EINES TAUGENICHTS

Sixth Printing, 1977

Copyright 1955 by Frederick Ungar Publishing Co.

PRINTED IN THE UNITED STATES OF AMERICA

Library of Congress Catalog Card Number: 55–8746

ISBN 0-8044-6134-1

Introduction

JOSEPH FREIHERR VON EICHENDORFF was born March 10, 1788 at Castle Lobowitz in Silesia, a short distance from Ratibor. At the age of ten he started a diary (the earliest stage at which any German poet is known to have begun as diarist of literature), and in 1805, at the age of seventeen, he began the university study of law at Halle. Later he studied at Heidelberg and Berlin, and in 1819 he passed with distinction the examination admitting him to full government service in a legal capacity. From 1816 to 1844 he held various administrative posts, a highly respected servant of the state. After his retirement he lived successively in Vienna, Berlin, Cöthen, and Dresden, and finally settled in Neisse, Silesia, where he died November 26, 1857.

Eichendorff's first published work was some poems which were printed in a magazine in 1808. Two years later he began a novel, *Ahnung und Gegenwart,* which came out in 1815. The novelette entitled *Aus dem Leben eines Taugenichts* was written in Königsberg and published in one volume with *Das Marmorbild* in 1826. Later publications, which were numerous, included verse epics, fairy tales, translations, scholarly works, and, above all, poetry. Many critics regard Eichendorff as the greatest German lyricist after Goethe, and his finest poems became popular in the best sense of the word; some of them are still widely current as folksongs. Our story includes several outstanding lyrics.

Aus dem Leben eines Taugenichts, which is universally regarded as one of the brightest gems of German romanticism, may also be looked upon as a spiritual self-portrait of the author. From friends we know that Eichendorff was completely without vanity as regards his poetic creations, unspoiled and serene, yet quite aware of his own talents and merits. Just such a character is assigned to the "good-for-nothing" of his story. Naively self-conscious, wholly candid about his shortcomings, light-hearted and optimistic, incredibly stupid at times and nevertheless lovable, this unnamed young man sings and fiddles his way through the entire tale in the rose-tinted atmosphere of an earthly paradise in the springtime. Not a drop of rain falls in this world, the sun shines every day, and the nights are ablaze with full moons and twinkling stars. It is a romantic love which permeates the human scene as the scent of orange blossoms fills the night air in a flowering grove. These lovers are passionately devoted to each other, but it is a passion which, like sunshine at dawn, gives light without heat. There is just one kiss in the whole story and even that is more friendly than ardent.

It is part of the charm of romantic fantasy that it is completely unrealistic. This story is a fairy tale without fairies, so to speak. When the hero gets into a fix, something or somebody comes to the rescue without his needing to give it much if any thought. Happy coincidence is a stage property which is so unobtrusively employed that only upon reflection do we discover all its workings. Moreover, human nature is here seen at its best; there are odd characters but no bad ones, freaks but no villains. A spy makes a brief appearance, but he is merely a plot requisite, and his interference is of no avail and has no importance.

Indispensable to true romanticism, it seems to me, is true poetry, and in that respect our story is unsurpassed. Indeed, it might fairly be called a prose poem, not so much with respect to its form, although many of the sentences have an incomparable music, as to the imaginative spirit which informs the entire narrative. The author's inventiveness in leading us through one happy scene after another is comparable to the composition of a poetic cycle or sequence, in which each lyric, independent in itself, is linked to and gains significance from its neighbors on either side of it. The magic of words has seldom been more happily demonstrated.

B. Q. M.

PRINCIPAL DATES OF EICHENDORFF'S LIFE

March 10, 1788 Born in Castle Lubowitz (Silesia).

1805–08 Study of law at Halle and Heidelberg.

1808 Poems in *Zeitschrift für Wissenschaft und Kunst*.

1809 Study in Berlin.

1810–13 Study in Vienna.

1813 Army service.

1814 Marriage to Luise von Larisch.

1815 *Ahnung und Gegenwart* (romance).

1816 Breslau, government service.

1821 Transfer to Danzig.

1823 Transfer to Berlin.

1824 Transfer to Königsberg.

1826 *Aus dem Leben eines Taugenichts, Das Marmorbild* (novelettes).

1828 *Ezelin von Romano* (tragedy).

1830 *Der letzte Held von Marienburg* (tragedy).

1831 Transfer to Berlin.

1833 *Die Freier* (comedy).

1837 *Das Schloß Dürande* (novelette.

1837 *Gedichte*.

1844 Retirement.

1846–55 Shifts of residence.

1846–53 *Geistliche Schauspiele* (translations of Calderon).

November 26, 1857 Death at Neisse (Silesia).

Chapter One

ONCE AGAIN the wheel of my father's mill was lustily splashing and clashing, the snow was busily dripping from the roof, and the sparrows were twittering and fluttering about; I was sitting on the doorsill and wiping the sleep out of my eyes; I felt utterly contented in the warm sunshine. Suddenly my father came out; he had been making a rumpus in the mill since daybreak, and his nightcap sat awry on his head. He said to me,

"You good-for-nothing! There you are sunning yourself again, stretching your bones till they ache, and letting me do all the work alone. I can't feed you here any longer. Spring is at hand: go out into the world for once and earn your own living."

"Well," said I, "if I am a good-for-nothing, that's all right with me; I'll go out into the world and make my fortune." And really I was quite pleased, for only a short while before I had had a notion to go traveling, hearing the yellowhammer, which all through the autumn and winter had kept chirping mournfully outside the window, "Farmer, hire me; farmer, hire me!" now in the lovely springtime calling quite proudly and merrily from the big tree, "Farmer, keep your work!"

So I went into the house, and from the wall I took down my fiddle, which I could play quite nicely, my father gave me a few pennies for the road, and I sauntered away down the long village street. I was secretly filled with delight, seeing all my old acquaintances and companions going out to right and left, digging and ploughing, just the same as all other days, while I was free to rove out into the world. In no little pride and contentment I shouted "Goodby!" to the poor folks on all sides, but nobody paid much attention. I felt as if there were an endless Sunday within me. And when I finally got out among the open fields, I took out my beloved fiddle and played and sang as I walked along the highway:

> Whom God would show the highest favor,
> He sends into the world to rove;
> He grants him every wondrous savor
> Of stream and field and hill and grove.
>
> The dullards in their houses lying
> Are not refreshed by morning's red:
> They only know of babies crying,
> Of burdens, cares, and daily bread.
>
> The brooklets from the hills are springing,
> The larks are soaring high with zest:
> Why should not I join in their singing
> With open throat and joyous breast?
>
> To God I leave the rule unswerving:
> Who brooks and larks and wood and fell
> And earth and heaven is preserving,
> Will safely guide my course as well.

Presently I looked around and saw an elegant coach coming quite close to me; no doubt it had been following me for some little time without my noticing it, my heart being so full of music, for it was moving quite slowly, and two aristocratic ladies were thrusting their heads out of the carriage and listening to me. One was especially beautiful and younger than the other, but I really liked them both. When I stopped singing, the older one halted the carriage and addressed me very graciously, saying, "Well, merry fellow, you can sing very pretty songs!" Said I, not too slow, "Please your ladyship, I could sing much nicer ones." So then she said in return, "And where are you bound for so early in the morning?" But I was ashamed of not knowing that myself, and I said boldly, "To Vienna," whereupon they conversed in a foreign tongue that I did not understand. The younger one shook her head several times, but the other one just laughed all the time, and finally she called out to me, "You just jump on behind, for we are going to Vienna too."

Who was more pleased than I? I made an obeisance and with one jump landed behind the carriage, the coachman cracked his whip, and we flew along the gleaming road till the wind whistled around my hat.

And now behind me sank village, gardens, and church steeples, before me rose up new villages, castles, and mountains, while below me crops, bushes, and meadows sped past pell-mell, and above me were countless larks in the clear blue air—I felt ashamed to cry aloud, but inwardly I was shouting, and I danced and pranced so wildly on the carriage-step that I nearly lost the fiddle from under my arm. But as the sun climbed ever higher, as heavy white midday clouds rose up all around the horizon, and everything in the air and on the wide landscape grew so empty and still and sultry above the gently waving grain, then for the first time I again recalled my village and my father and our mill, how cozy and cool it was there by the shady pond, and thought how very far all that now lay behind me. It gave me such an odd feeling, as if I must turn around again; I thrust my fiddle in between coat and vest, seated myself, deep in thought, on the footboard, and fell asleep.

When I opened my eyes, the carriage was standing still under tall lindens, behind which a broad flight of steps led between columns up to a splendid castle. Looking sidewards through the trees I saw the spires of Vienna. The ladies, as it seemed, had long since got out, and the horses were unhitched. I was greatly startled at suddenly finding myself all alone, and I swiftly dashed into the castle, hearing laughter ring out from an upper window.

I had a strange time in this castle. First, as I gaped about in the wide, cool vestibule, somebody tapped me on the shoulder with a stick. I whirled around, and there stood a tall gentleman in gala dress, with a broad bandoleer of gold and silver hanging down to his hips, with a silver-knobbed staff in his hand and an extraordinarily long, hooked, princely nose in his face, and he as big and magnificent as a puffed-up turkey cock; he asked me what I wanted there. I was quite taken aback and for sheer fright and astonishment could not get out a word. Thereupon several lackeys came running from upstairs and downstairs; they said nothing, merely looked me up and down. Next a lady's maid (as I afterward heard she was) walked right up to me and said: that I was a charming boy, and her mistress wanted to know whether I would like to take service here as gardener's helper.

I felt in my vest, but my few pennies were gone, and must have jumped out of my pocket when I was prancing on the footboard; so I had nothing but my fiddleplaying, for which, incidentally, the gentleman with the staff, as he remarked to me in passing, would not give a red cent. Hence in my utter fear I told the lady's maid "Yes," still eyeing askance that uncanny figure which oscillated back and forth in the hall like the pendulum of a tower clock, and which even now was emerging from the background, majestic and awe-inspiring. Last of all came the gardener, who muttered in his beard something about rabble and clodhopper and led me to the garden, meanwhile delivering to me a lengthy sermon: how I should always be sober and industrious, not go vagabonding about the world, not indulge in any breadless arts or other useless stuff, and then in due time I might get somewhere. There were some more very pretty, well-phrased, and useful teachings, but the trouble is that since then I have forgotten most of them. And anyway, I really haven't any idea how all this had come about, for I merely kept on saying "Yes" to everything. I felt just like a bird whose wings have been watered. And so, praise God, here I was a breadwinner!

It was nice to live in the garden; I had plenty of warm food every day and more money for wine than I needed; only unfortunately I did have a good deal to do. I also liked very much the temples, the arbors, the pretty green walks and all; I only wished I could have quietly gone strolling among them, holding sensible converse, like the gentlemen and ladies who came there every day. As often as the gardener was away and I was alone, I immediately pulled out my stubby pipe, sat myself down, and figured out polite and pretty speeches which I would use in conversing with that lovely young lady who had brought me to the castle—that is, if I were a cavalier and walking about here with her. Or on sultry afternoons I would lie down on my back, when all was so still that all you heard was the bees humming, and would watch the clouds above me sailing toward my village, or the grasses and flowers swaying to and fro, and would think of that lady, and then it would often happen that the lovely lady would really pass at a distance through the garden with a guitar or a book, as silent, tall, and friendly as an angel, so that I hardly knew whether I were dreaming or waking.

And so, as I once chanced to pass a summerhouse on my way to work, I was singing to myself:

> Where'er I look and wander,
> The fields and woodlands through,
> From hill to valley yonder,
> Sweet lady, I grow fonder
> And send my love to you!

Suddenly, between the half-open blinds and flowerpots of the cool, dark summerhouse, I saw the sparkle of two lovely, young, eager eyes. I was quite startled and did not finish the song, but continued on my way to work without looking back.

In the evening, it happening to be a Saturday, and I standing with my fiddle at the window of my garden house, looking forward to the pleasure of the coming Sunday and still thinking of the sparkling eyes, all at once the lady's maid came tripping through the twilight. "Here's a present for you from the lovely lady, so you can drink to her health. And a good night to you!"

6

With that she briskly set a bottle of wine on the sill and immediately disappeared again among the flowers and hedges like a lizard.

But I went on standing for a long time before the wonderful bottle and didn't know what to make of it. And if till then I had fiddled merrily, now I played and sang harder than ever, and sang the song about the lovely lady clear to the end, and all the other songs I knew, till all the nightingales outside awoke, while moon and stars had long since appeared above the garden. Ah, there was one good and lovely night!

There is no cradlesong that predicts the infant's future; sometimes a blind hen finds a grain of corn; he who laughs last laughs best; it's often the unexpected that happens; man proposes and God disposes. In such fashion I was meditating the next day, again sitting in the garden with my pipe, and, looking attentively down at my person, almost feeling as if I were nothing but a ragamuffin. Quite contrary to my usual habits, I was now getting up very early every day, even before the gardeners and the other workmen were stirring. It was so lovely out in the garden at that time. The flowers, the fountains, the rosebushes, and the entire garden sparkled in the morning sunshine like pure gold and jewels. And in the avenues of tall beeches it was then still as quiet, cool, and solemn as in a church, and only the birds were fluttering about and picking at the sand. Right in front of the castle, under the very windows where the lovely lady lived, there was a blossoming bush.

That was where I always went in the early morning, to crouch down behind the branches and look up at the windows from there, for I lacked the courage to show myself in the open. And thus it was that I saw that loveliest lady, day after day, come to the open window in her snow-white gown, still flushed and not fully awake. Now she would braid her dark brown hair, while her charmingly roving eyes took in shrubbery and garden, now she would stoop and tie up the plants that stood before her window, or she might even lay the guitar on her white arm and sing to it so wondrously out over the garden that even now, when one of those songs happens to come to mind, my heart is like to turn upside down for sadness —and oh, all that was long, long ago!

Things went on this way for more than a week. But one time she was again standing right at the window, and all was still round about, when a miserable fly got into my nose and I fell into a fearful fit of sneezing that I simply could not stop. She leaned far out of the window and saw me, wretch that I was, lurking behind the bush. Now I was embarrassed, and for many days I stayed away.

At last I ventured there again, but this time the window stayed shut; for four, five, six mornings I sat behind the bush, but she did not come to the window again. So then time hung heavy, and I took heart and every morning I walked bold as brass along the castle front and under all the windows. But always and always the dear and lovely lady was missing. A little farther on I always saw the other lady standing at the window. I had never got such a good look at her before. She was truly rosy and plump in a very handsome way, and quite splendid and haughty to look at, like a tulip. I always made her a low bow, and, I must say, she thanked me every time and nodded, and she blinked her eyes at me with quite extraordinary politeness. Only once I thought I observed that the lovely one was also standing at her window behind the curtain, peeping out from her concealment.

Many days, however, went by without my seeing her. She came no more to the garden, she came no more to the window. The gardener chided me for a lazy loafer, and I was peevish; my own nose was in my way when I looked out upon the untrammeled world of God.

So I was lying in the garden one Sunday afternoon, annoyed with myself, as I looked up into the blue smoke of my pipe, because I had not taken up some other trade, so that at least I too wouldn't have to look forward to a blue Monday on the next day. The other lads had meanwhile dolled themselves up and had all gone off to the dance halls in the neighboring suburb. Everybody was now surging and splurging in his Sunday best, out in the warm air among the bright houses and the roving barrel organs, flooding to and fro. But I was sitting like a bittern among the reeds of a solitary pond in the park, rocking in a skiff that was tied up there, while the vesper bells rang out from the city across the garden, and the swans floated slowly back and forth the water around us. I felt sad enough to die.

Presently I heard in the distance all sorts of voices, merry and jumbled speech and laughter, coming closer and closer, and then red and white scarves, hats, and plumes shimmered through the green, and all at once there came a lightsome, brightsome bevy of young gentlemen and ladies from the castle across the meadow towards me, with my two ladies in the midst of them. I got up and was about to leave, when the older of the two ladies spied me.

"Why, you're just the one we need," she cried out to me with laughing lips, "won't you row us across the pond to the opposite shore?"

Now the ladies got into the boat one after the other, cautiously and timidly, and the gentlemen helped them in and bragged a bit about their courage on the water. When all the ladies had seated themselves on the side benches, I pushed off from the shore. One of the young gentlemen, standing close to the bow, began imperceptibly to rock the boat. Then the ladies twisted their bodies anxiously this way and that, and some even shrieked. The lovely lady, who was holding a lily in her hand, sat close by the edge of the boat and looked with a quiet smile down into the water, which she touched with the lily, so that her entire image was once more to be seen between the reflected clouds and trees in the water, like an angel floating softly across the deep blue ground of the sky.

Now as I was looking at her thus, it suddenly occurred to the other one of my ladies, the jolly, plump one, that I might sing her something during the boatride. Quickly a very dainty young gentleman, with glasses on his nose, who was sitting next to her, turned around, softly kissed her hand, and said, "I thank you for that ingenious idea! A folksong, sung by the folk in open fields and woods, is like an Alpine violet on the Alps—these anthologies are only herbariums—it is the soul of the national soul." But I said that I did not know anything that was fine enough for such lords and ladies. Then the saucy lady's maid, who was standing close to me with a basket full of cups and bottles, and whom I had not noticed at all till then, spoke up: "Oh, you know a very pretty little song about a lovely lady."

"Yes, yes, just sing that out good and loud," cried the lady again.

I turned red all over. But now the lovely lady, too, lifted her eyes from the water all at once and gave me a look that pierced body and soul. So then I hesitated no longer, but took heart, and sang with gusto and with all my might:

Where'er I look and wander,
The fields and woodlands through,
From hill to valley yonder,
Sweet lady, I grow fonder
And send my love to you!

Within my garden finding
Sweet flowers, fine and rare,
Full many a wreath I'm winding,
And loving thoughts I'm binding
With greetings for my fair.

No wreath may I deliver,
She dwells too high above;
The flowers in death must quiver,
And all that I can give her
Is my unending love.

I may seem gay and merry,
And still I work and slave;
I gaily sing, O very,
With bursting heart I'll bury
Myself in my own grave.

The boat grounded, and all the company got out; many of the young gentlemen, as I had plainly observed, had made fun of me to the ladies, while I was singing, with sly looks and whispers. The gentleman with the glasses took me by the hand as he went away and said something, I have forgotten just what, and the older one of my two ladies looked very kindly at me. During my whole song the lovely lady had kept her eyes lowered, and now she too went away and said nothing at all. But I had tears in my eyes even while I was still singing, and now the song made my heart ready to burst for shame and for pain: all at once it came over me so clearly, how that she is so lovely and I so poor and despised and forsaken by the world—and when they had all disappeared behind the bushes, I could restrain myself no longer, but flung myself down in the grass and wept bitterly.

Chapter Two

CLOSE BESIDE our park ran the highway, only sepa-
rated from it by a high wall. A very neat tollhouse
with a red tile roof had been built there, and behind it
there was a small, gaily fenced flower garden, which
was connected by means of a gap in the wall with the
shadiest and most secluded part of the castle park. The
tollkeeper, who had been inhabiting all this, had just
died. Early one morning, while I was still in the
deepest sleep, the clerk from the castle came to me
and summoned me in a great hurry to the bailiff. I
dressed quickly and sauntered along behind the merry
clerk, who picked a flower here and another there, as
he walked along, and pinned them to his lapel, or who
would make artful passes in the air with his swagger
cane, rattling off all kinds of talk to me and the breeze,
of which however I did not understand a word, because my eyes and ears were still full of sleep.

When I entered the office, where it was not yet even
fully light, the magistrate, from behind a monstrous
inkwell and piles of papers and books, looked at me
out of an impressive wig, like an owl peering from its
nest, and began, "What's your name? Where from?
Can you read, write, and reckon?" When I affirmed
this, he replied, "Well, in consideration of your good
conduct and particular merits the mistress is bestowing
on you the vacant post of tollkeeper." I hastily re-

viewed in my mind my previous conduct and manners, and I had to admit that ultimately I myself would say that the bailiff was right. And so here I was actually a tollkeeper before I knew it.

At once I moved into my new dwelling, and in a short time I had fixed it up. I had found various effects that the late incumbent had bequeathed to his successor, among them a gorgeous red dressing gown with yellow dots, green slippers, a nightcap, and some long-stemmed pipes. All these were things I had wished for even when I was living at home, where I used to see our pastor going about so comfortably. All day long, therefore (there was nothing else to do), I sat on the little bench in front of my house in dressing gown and nightcap, smoked the longest pipe that I had inherited from my lamented predecessor, and watched the people walking, driving, and riding on the highway. I only wished that some of the people from my village, who had always said I'd never come to anything in all my life, might also come by some time and see me like that.

The dressing gown was becoming to me, and the whole business was very much to my liking. So I would sit there and think various thoughts: how hard all beginnings are, and how a more stylish life is really very comfortable, and privately I resolved to forswear all traveling, to save up money like others, and in time without doubt to reach some distinguished goal in life. Meantime, however, for all my resolves, cares, and occupations, I was far from forgetting that most lovely lady.

The potatoes and other vegetables that I had found in my little garden I threw out, filling it with the choicest flowers, whereat the hall porter at the

14

castle with the great and princely nose, who often came to see me, now that I was living here, and had become an intimate friend of mine, eyed me askance and took me for a person whom good fortune had robbed of sense. But I did not let that disturb me. For not far away in the castle park I could hear dainty voices speaking, among which I thought I recognized that of my lovely lady, although the dense shrubbery prevented my seeing anybody. Every day, then, I tied up a bouquet of the prettiest flowers I had, climbed at evening over the wall, when it grew dark, and laid it on a stone table in the middle of an arbor; and every evening, when I took the new bouquet there, the old one was gone from the table.

One evening the company had ridden out hunting; the sun was just setting, covering the entire land with glamor and glory, the Danube wound off into the distance in splendor, as if made of gold and silver, and from all the hillsides the vintners were singing and shouting far across the land. I was sitting with the porter on the little bench in front of my house, enjoying, in the mild air, the way the lights and sounds of the merry day died away before us. Then all at once the horns of the returning hunters could be heard from afar, giving each other tuneful answer, from time to time, from the opposite hills. I was delighted to the bottom of my heart, and I sprang up and cried out, as if enchanted and carried away with pleasure, "Ah, there's a calling for me, the noble hunt!"

But the porter quietly knocked the ashes from his pipe and said, "That's what *you* think. I've gone along too, but you hardly earn the soles you wear out; and you never get rid of coughs and colds, that's from everlastingly wet feet." I don't know how it was, but a silly rage came over me, so that my whole body fairly trembled. All at once the entire fellow with his monotonous cloak, his everlasting feet, his tobacco snuffing, his big nose and everything, was detestable to me. As if beside myself, I seized him by the breast and said, "Porter, you get along home now, or I'll beat you up this instant!" At these words the porter was overcome by his former notion that I had gone mad. He looked at me dubiously and with secret fear, freed himself from my clutch without saying a word, and walked, still looking fearfully back at me, with long strides to the castle, where he breathlessly announced that I had now really become a raving maniac.

But finally I couldn't help bursting out laughing and was thoroughly glad to be rid of the wiseacre, for it was just the time at which I was always wont to put my bouquet in the arbor. Today too I quickly jumped over the wall, and I was just making for the stone table when I heard hoofbeats at some distance. I could no longer escape, for already my sweet and lovely lady herself was coming along, in a green riding habit and with nodding plumes on her hat, riding slowly and, it seemed, in deep thought down the bridlepath. I felt exactly as in the former days, when I had read in the old books at my father's house the story of the beautiful Magelone, how she would come out from under the tall trees amid the ever approaching notes of the bugles and the shifting lights of evening. I could not budge from the spot. But she started violently, as she suddenly caught sight of me, and halted almost involuntarily. I was as if intoxicated with fear, heartthrobs, and great joy, and seeing that she was really wearing on her breast my bouquet of yesterday, I could restrain myself no longer, but said in utter confusion, "Sweet and lovely lady, take from me this bouquet too, and all the flowers from my garden, and all that I have. Oh, if I could only go through fire for you!" Right at the beginning she had eyed me so seriously and almost angrily that her look pierced me to the marrow, but then, so long as I was speaking, she kept her eyes lowered. Just now some riders and voices could be heard in the thicket. Swiftly she snatched the bouquet from my hand and soon thereafter, without saying a word, she had disappeared at the other end of the shaded path.

From that evening on I had neither rest nor peace. Constantly I felt as I always had when the spring was about to begin, so restless and happy, yet without knowing why, as if some great fortune or some other extraordinary thing were impending. In particular, I could no longer manage that miserable figuring, and when the greenish golden sunshine came through the chestnut tree outside the window and fell on the figures, shifting so quickly from balance forward to total sum, and again adding up and down, I would have strange notions, so that sometimes I became quite confused and actually could not count up to three. For the 8 would keep on looking to me like my stout, tight-laced lady with the wide coiffure, while the "naughty seven" was like a road sign pointing backward, or like a gallows. I had the most fun with 9, which would so often stand on its head before I was aware of it and become a 6, whereas the 2, resembling a question mark, would have such a quizzical look, as if to ask me, "Where will this finally take you, you poor zero? Without her, that slender one and all, you'll never be anything but a naught!"

Even to sit in front of my door no longer afforded

me any pleasure. To make myself more comfortable I would carry out a footstool and stretch out my feet on it, and I patched up an old sunshade left in the house and stuck it up over me like a Chinese pavilion to keep off the sun. But it did no good. It seemed to me, as I went on sitting and smoking and ruminating, that my legs were gradually getting longer and longer out of sheer boredom, and that lack of work was making my nose grow out, when I looked down it for hours at a time. And then when at times a post chaise would come along before daybreak, and a dainty little face, of which nothing but the sparkling eyes could be seen in the dim light, would lean curiously out of the coach and amiably bid me good morning, while in the villages around about the crowing of the cocks sounded so fresh as it came to me across the fields of waving grain, and among the dawn-lit wisps of cloud high up in the sky some larks that had waked too early were already soaring about, and then the postillion would take his bugle and drive on, blowing and blowing—then I would stand there a long time and look after the coach, feeling just as if I must travel off with it on the spot, and go far, far off into the world.

I still laid my bouquets, every day, as soon as the sun went down, on the stone table in the dark arbor. But that was just the trouble: from that evening on everything was over. Not a soul paid any attention to them: as often as I took a look in the early morning, there the flowers were still lying as on the day before, looking at me in positive melancholy with their wilted, drooping heads dotted with dew, as if they were weeping. That vexed me greatly. I stopped tying up bouquets. And now the weeds might flourish in my garden as much as they would, and I simply let the flowers stand and grow until the wind blew the petals away. For in my heart too everything looked just as wild and mixed up and spoiled.

Now, at this critical juncture it so happened that one time, just as I was lying by the window of my house and peevishly looking out into the empty air, the lady's maid from the castle came tripping across the road. When she caught sight of me, she quickly turned in at my house and stopped in front of the window. "The master came back from his journey yesterday," she said precipitately. "He did?" I answered in surprise, for I had paid no attention to anything for some weeks and did not even know that he had been away. "Then the young mistress his daughter must have been very much pleased."

The maid looked oddly at me from head to foot, so that I had to think hard to be sure I hadn't said something stupid. "You certainly don't know anything at all," she said at last, turning up her little nose. "Well," she went on, "this evening there's to be dancing in the castle in the master's honor, and a masquerade. My mistress will be masked, too, and dressed as a gardener's wife—you understand—as a gardener's wife. Now my mistress has observed that you have especially pretty flowers in your garden."

"That's funny," I thought to myself, "you can hardly see the flowers for the weeds any more."

But she went on, "Now as my mistress needs pretty flowers for her costume, and fresh ones that have just been picked, you are to bring her some, and this evening, when it has grown dark, you are to wait with them under the great pear tree in the park, and she will come and get the flowers."

I was quite taken aback with joy at this announcement, and in my delight I rushed away from the window and out to the lady's maid.

"Ugh, the filthy dressing gown!" cried she, seeing me all at once in my outfit in the open air. That annoyed me, and unwilling to be backward in gallantry, I cut some pretty capers in an effort to catch and kiss her. But unfortunately the dressing gown, which was much too long for me, got tangled up under my feet, and I fell full length on the ground. By the time I had picked myself up again, the lady's maid was already far away, and even from that distance I heard her laugh so that she had to hold her sides.

But now I had something to dream about and look forward to. Then she was still mindful of me and my flowers! I went into my garden and hurriedly pulled all the weeds out of the beds and flung them high over my head into the shimmering air, as if I were pulling all troubles and griefs out by the roots. Now the roses were again like her mouth, the sky-blue convolvulus like her eyes, and the snow-white lily with its sadly drooping little head looked exactly like her. I laid them carefully in a little basket. It was a quiet, lovely evening, without a cloud in the sky. Some stars were already appearing on the canopy above, from afar the murmurs of the Danube could be heard coming across the fields, in the tall trees of the castle park beside me countless birds were merrily singing together. Oh, I was so happy!

When night finally fell, I hung my basket on my arm and set out for the great park. In the basket everything was so gaily and charmingly mingled, white, red, and blue, and fragrant, that my heart fairly laughed whenever I peeped in.

Full of happy thoughts I walked in the lovely moonlight through the quiet paths, neatly strewn with sand, across the little white bridges, under which the swans were floating on the water in their sleep, and past the dainty arbors and summer-houses. I soon found out which was the great pear tree, for it was the same one under which, when I was still a gardener's helper, I had been wont to lie on sultry afternoons.

Here it was so lonesome and dark. Only a tall aspen kept on quivering and whispering with its silvery leaves. From the castle one could hear the dance music now and then. I also heard human voices at times in the park; often they came quite close to me, and then all at once it would be quite still again.

My heart throbbed. I felt eery and strange, as if I were planning to rob somebody. For a long time I stood leaning stock-still against the tree, listening in all directions, but as nobody seemed to be coming I could stand it no longer. I hung my basket on my arm and quickly climbed up into the pear tree, so as once more to draw my breath in the open air.

Once up there, I could hear the dance music better than ever across the tree tops. I could survey the whole park and look straight into the brightly lighted windows of the castle. There the chandeliers were slowly revolving like garlands of stars, while countless gaily dressed gentlemen and ladies, as in a shadow play, were weaving and waltzing and whirling around each other, in an unrecognizable medley; now and then some of them would settle down at a window and look down into the park. But out in front of the castle the lawns, the shrubbery, and the trees looked as if gilded by the many lights in the ballroom, so that both birds and flowers fairly seemed to wake up out of sleep. Farther around me and behind me the park lay all black and still.

"There she is dancing now," I thought to myself up there in the tree, "and has no doubt long since forgotten you and your flowers again. Everybody is so merry, and nobody cares about you. And that is my lot always and everywhere. Each one has his plot of ground staked out, has his warm stove, his cup of coffee, his wife, his glass of wine in the evening, and is thoroughly content; even the hall porter feels quite happy inside his tall body. For me there's no happiness anywhere. It's as if I had always come just too late, as if the entire world had not counted me in at all."

As I was philosophizing thus, I suddenly heard an approaching rustle in the grass. Two dainty voices were conversing very softly and very near by. Soon the branches of the shrubs were pushed apart, and the lady's maid thrust her tiny little face into the summer arbor, peering about in every direction. The moonlight sparkled brightly in her cunning eyes, as they peeped out. I held my breath and kept staring down. Nor was it long until the gardeneress, just as the lady's maid had described her to me the day before, actually stepped out from between the trees. My heart throbbed to bursting. But she had a mask on and looked around the place in surprise, as it seemed to me. And now I got the impression that she was not at all slender and dainty. At last she stepped quite close to the tree and took off her mask. It was, upon my word, that other and older gracious lady!

How glad I was, now that I had recovered from my first fright, that I was up here in safety. "How in all the world," I thought, "did she get here now? And if my dear, gracious, lovely lady comes to get her flowers—that will be a pretty mess!" I could have fairly shed tears of vexation at this entire muddle.

Meantime the counterfeit gardeneress down below began to talk: "It is so suffocatingly hot up there in the ballroom, I just had to go and cool off a bit in this lovely outdoor world of nature." And she fanned herself incessantly with her mask and blew the air away from herself. By the bright moonlight I could plainly see how the cords on her neck were fairly puffed out and swollen; she looked thoroughly vexed and was brick-red in the face. Meantime the lady's maid was looking about behind all the hedges, as if she had lost a pin.

"I simply must have fresh flowers for my costume," the lady went on again, "where can he be keeping himself!" The lady's maid went on looking, secretly giggling to herself all the time. "Did you say something, Rosette?" asked the lady sharply.

"I say what I have always said," replied the lady's maid, putting on a very serious and ingenuous expression, "that tollkeeper is and will always be a booby, and I'll wager he's lying asleep behind some bush or other."

I felt in all my limbs an itch to jump down and save my reputation—when all at once one could hear a great drumming and musicking and shouting up at the castle.

Now the gardeneress could wait no longer. She started up peevishly: "There the company is going to salute the master. Come, we shall be missed!" And with that she quickly put her mask back on and furiously walked away with the lady's maid toward the castle. The trees and bushes seemed to be pointing oddly at her with long noses and fingers, the moonlight danced nimbly up and down her broad back as on a keyboard, and so she swiftly took her exit, just as I had sometimes seen singers do on the stage, to the sound of trumpets and drums.

But I hardly knew, up there in my tree, what to make of it all, and now kept my eyes unswervingly fixed on the castle; for a circle of tall lanterns down at the foot of the entrance steps cast a strange glow from there upon the flashing windows and far out into the park. It was the servants, who were just in the act of serenading their young master. In the midst of them the hall porter, looking in all his finery like a minister of state, stood before a music stand, wrestling for dear life with a bassoon.

Just as I was placing myself so as to listen to the pretty serenade, the French doors leading onto the upper balcony of the castle suddenly opened wide. A tall gentleman, handsome and stately looking, dressed in a uniform with many sparkling stars on it, stepped out on the balcony, leading by the hand the young sweet lovely lady, all in white, like a lily in the night, or as if the moon were sailing across the clear firmament.

I could not take my eyes from the spot, and park, trees, and fields sank out of reach of my senses, as she stood there so wondrously illuminated by the torches, tall and slender, now talking charmingly with the handsome officer, now nodding amiably down at the musicians. The people down below were beside themselves with joy, and finally I too no longer restrained myself and shouted "Vivat!" over and over with all my might.

But when she vanished again from the balcony, soon after that, and down below one torch after another went out, and the music stands were cleared away, and now the park round about me grew dark again and murmured as before—then I suddenly saw everything—then all at once it came upon me like a blow that in reality it was only the aunt who had sent for me to bring the flowers, that the lovely one was not thinking of me at all and had long since been married, and that I myself was a great fool.

All this plunged me into a veritable abyss of reflection. I wrapped myself like a porcupine in the sharp spines of my own thoughts: from the castle the dance-music rang out but rarely now, and the clouds wandered lonesomely across the dark garden and away. And so I sat up there in the tree like a night owl among the ruins of my happiness, the whole night through.

The cool air of morning woke me at last from my reveries. I was positively astonished as I suddenly looked about me. Music and dancing were long since ended, and in the castle and all around on the lawns, on the stone steps and pillars, everything looked so still, cool, and solemn; only the fountain at the entrance continued its lonely splashing. Here and there in the branches near me the birds were already awaking, shaking out their gay feathers, and eyeing their strange sleep-mate with curiosity and surprise as they spread their little wings. Gaily roving beams of the morning sun sparkled across the park and struck my breast.

Then I stood high up in my tree, and for the first time in a long while I looked far, far out across the land, seeing how single boats were already sailing down the Danube between the vineyards, and how the highways, still deserted, flung themselves over the shimmering land and far across the mountains and valleys like bridges.

I don't know how it came about—but all at once the wanderlust of former days seized upon me again: all the old melancholy and joy, and the great expectation. At the same time the thought came to me of how the lovely lady, up there in the castle, was now sleeping amid flowers and under silken covers, and an angel was sitting beside her on the bed in the morning silence. "No," I cried out, "I must away from here, and on and on, as far as the skies are blue!"

And with that I took my basket and flung it high in the air, so that it really was a pretty sight, the way the flowers fell through the branches and lay about in their bright colors on the green turf below. Then I myself descended quickly and went through the silent park to my dwelling. Time after time I would stand still here or there at some spot where I had once seen her, or where I had lain in the shade and thought of her.

In and around my house everything still looked just as I had left it the day before. The little garden was plundered and desolate, inside the room the great account-book still lay opened out, and my fiddle, which I had almost forgotten, hung all dusty on the wall. But a morning ray just shot through the opposite window and fell flashing on its strings. That rang in my heart like real music. "Yes," said I, "come here to me, faithful instrument! Our kingdom is not of this world!"

And so I took the fiddle from the wall, let account book, dressing gown, slippers, pipes, and parasol be as they were, and wandered, as poor as I had come, out of my little house and onto the shining highroad and away.

I looked back many times; I had such strange feelings, so sad and yet again so excessively joyful, like a bird that escapes from its cage. And when I had already gone a long way, I brought forward my fiddle, out there in the open, and sang:

> To God I leave the rule unswerving:
> Who brooks and larks and wood and fell
> And earth and heaven is preserving,
> Will safely guide my course as well!

The castle, the park, and the spires of Vienna had already dropped out of sight behind me in the morning haze, over me countless larks were jubilating high in the air; so I marched along between the green hills and past cheerful towns and villages, down to Italy.

Chapter Three

BUT HERE was a state of things! I had given no thought whatever to the fact that I didn't really know the right way to go. Nor was there to be seen far and wide, in the quiet morning hour, anybody whom I could have asked, and not far from me the highroad forked into many new highways, which led far, far away over the highest mountains, as if they would take one out of the world, so that I felt fairly dizzy when I looked hard at them.

At last a peasant came along the road, going to church, I think, as it chanced to be Sunday, wearing an old-fashioned greatcoat with large silver buttons and carrying a long Spanish cane with a very massive silver knob on it, which flashed in the sunlight a long way off. I asked him at once with much politeness, "Can you tell me which road goes to Italy?" The peasant stopped short, looked at me, bethought himself with greatly protruding underlip, and looked at me again. I said once more, "To Italy, where the oranges grow."

"What do I care about your oranges!" said the peasant, and strode stoutly on his way again. I should have expected him to have better manners, for he looked very stately.

What was to be done now? Turn around again and go back to my village? Then the folks would have pointed their fingers at me, and the youngsters would have pranced around me: "Well, a thousand welcomes on your return from the great world! How do things look out in the great world? Didn't you bring us some ginger-cookies from the great world?" The hall porter with the princely nose, who indeed knew much about world history, had often said to me, "Worthy and esteemed Mr. Tollkeeper! Italy is a beautiful country: there the dear God looks after everything, there you can lie down on your back in the sunshine and the raisins will grow right into your mouth, and if the tarantula bites you, then you will dance with uncommon agility, even if you haven't ever learned how to dance."

"No, to Italy, to Italy!" I cried with glee, and without thinking about different ways to go I ran forward on the road that happened to get under my feet.

When I had thus gone some distance, I saw a very pretty orchard to the right of the road, where the morning sun shimmered so merrily in between the trunks and the tops of the trees that it looked as if the turf were spread with golden rugs. Seeing nobody, I climbed over the low fence and laid myself very comfortably in the grass under an apple tree, for all my bones were aching from the night I had spent in the tree. From there one could see far across the land, and as it was a Sunday, the peal of bells came over the quiet fields from the greatest distance, and everywhere the country folk were walking to church in their Sunday best through fields and bushes. I was very merry at heart, the birds sang above me in the tree, I thought of my mill and of the garden of the lovely lady, and how all that was now so far, far away—until at last

I fell asleep. Then in a dream it seemed to me that the lovely lady was coming toward me from the glorious landscape below, only she was really flying slowly amid the peal of the bells, with long white veils that floated out in the morning-glow. And then again it seemed as if we were not away off in the world, but in the deep shadows by the mill near my village. But everything was silent and deserted there, as when the people are all at church on a Sunday, and only the sound of the organ comes to you through the trees— so that it fairly made my heart ache. But the lovely lady was very kind and pleasant, she held me by the hand and walked with me and sang unceasingly in this solitude the pretty song that she always used to sing to the guitar in the early mornings by the open window of the castle, and I kept seeing her image in the quiet pond, only many thousand times lovelier, but with strangely large eyes, which looked at me so rigidly that I could almost have felt afraid. Then all the once the mill began to work, at first in single, slow pulsations, then roaring ever faster and louder, and the pond grew dark and agitated, the lovely lady turned quite pale, and her veils became longer and longer and fluttered horribly in long tails like wisps of fog high up to the sky; the roaring kept on increasing, and often it seemed as if now and then the hall porter were blowing notes on his bassoon, so that at last I woke up with violent palpitation of the heart.

A breeze had actually arisen and was blowing softly through the apple tree above me; but that which was making such a roar and noise was neither the mill nor the hall porter, but the same peasant who had previously refused to show me the way to Italy. But he had taken off his Sunday coat and stood before me in a white smock. "Well," said he, as I was still wiping the sleep out of my eyes, "are you thinking of picking up some oranges here, trampling down my nice grass instead of going to church, you lazybones!"

I was merely vexed that this boor had waked me up. I sprang up quite indignantly and promptly replied, "What, you want to call me down, do you? I was a gardener before you ever thought of it, and a tollkeeper, and if you had ever driven to town you'd have had to take off your greasy nightcap to me, and I had a house of my own and a red dressing-gown with yellow dots."

But the clodhopper cared nothing for that, but put his arms akimbo and merely said, "What do you want? hey! hey!" And now I saw that he was really a short, stocky, bowlegged fellow, with staring pop-eyes and a red and somewhat crooked nose. And as he kept on saying nothing but hey—hey!—each time taking one step closer to me, all at once I was seized with such a queer and horrible fear that I quickly took to my heels, leaped over the fence, and, without looking around, kept on running across country, so that the fiddle resounded in its case.

When I finally came to a stop again in order to catch my breath, the orchard and the whole valley were out of sight, and I was standing in a fine forest. But I paid little attention to that, for now the whole rumpus annoyed me more than ever, and the fact that the fellow talked so disrespectfully to me, and for a long time I kept on scolding to myself. Occupied with such thoughts, I walked along rapidly and got farther and farther away from the highway and into the heart of the mountains. The wood road on which I had been going along came to an end, and before me

I only had a narrow and little traveled footpath. All round there was nobody to be seen and no sound to be heard. But otherwise it was very delightful walking, for the tree-tops murmured and the birds sang very beautifully. So I commended myself to the guidance of God, pulled out my violin, and played over all my favorite pieces, so that it had a very merry sound in the solitary forest.

But this playing couldn't keep on forever, either, for every moment I would stumble over the miserable tree roots, and at last I began to be hungry, and still the forest refused to come to an end. So I roved at random all day long, and the sun was already shining aslant through the tree trunks, when I finally came out into a little grassy valley which was wholly enclosed by mountains and was full of red and yellow flowers, over which innumerable butterflies were fluttering about in the golden evening night. Here it was as solitary as if the world of men were a hundred miles away. Only the crickets chirped, and a herdsman lay over yonder in the tall grass and blew so sadly on his reed pipe that it was like to make your heart burst with grief. "Ah," I thought to myself, "if one could have as good a life as such a loafer! Chaps like me have to knock about the world and be always on the alert." As a clear and pretty little stream, which I could not cross, lay between us, I called out to him to ask where the nearest village was. But he did not disturb himself, merely stuck his head up out of the grass a little, pointed with his pipe toward the opposite forest, and calmly went on with his piping.

Meanwhile I marched forward briskly, for the light was already dimming. The birds, which had all set up a great outcry when the last rays of the sun gleamed through the forest, grew still all of a sudden, and I almost began to feel afraid in the everlasting, lonely murmuring of the woods. At last I heard the distant barking of dogs. I strode on faster, the woods lightened more and more, and soon thereafter I looked through the last of the trees and saw a lovely green, upon which many children were noisily romping about a great linden tree, which stood right in the middle of it. Farther along on the edge of the green was a tavern, before which some peasants were sitting around a table, playing cards and smoking. In front of the door on the other side young lads and girls were sitting, the latter with their arms wrapped in their aprons, chatting together in the cool of evening.

I made a quick decision, drew my fiddle from its case, and swiftly played a jolly country dance as I advanced from the woods. The girls were surprised, and the old men laughed till the echoes went far into the forest. But when I had kept on this way as far as the linden tree, and now leaned my back against it and kept on playing, a subdued murmur and whispering set in among the young folks to right and left, the boys finally laid down their Sunday pipes, each one seized his girl, and before I knew it the young peasant folk were whirling lustily around me, with dogs barking, smocks flying, and the children standing around me in a circle and looking curiously up into my face and then at the fingers I was moving so nimbly.

When the first waltz was done, I could tell better than ever how good music gets into your bones. The peasant boys, who had been lolling on the benches a moment before, with pipes in their mouths and their legs outstretched, were now suddenly transformed;

they let their gay-colored kerchiefs dangle at full length from their buttonholes, and capered about the girls so artfully that it was a real pleasure to see. One of them, who thought pretty well of himself, fished in his vest pocket for a long time, so the others should see it, and finally pulled out a small silver piece, which he tried to force into my hand. This vexed me, even though I had no money in my pocket at the moment. I told him he could keep his pennies, that I was merely playing for joy at being among people once more. But soon after that a nice-looking girl came to me with a great goblet of wine. "Musicians like to drink," she said with a little laugh, and her pearly teeth gleamed charmingly between her red lips, so that I should have liked to kiss them. She dipped her little mouth in the wine, while her eyes flashed at me across the top of the glass, and then handed the goblet to me. I drained the glass and then played afresh, so that everyone went whirling merrily around me.

Meanwhile the old men had quit their game, and the young folk also began to tire and scattered, and so bit by bit it grew quite silent and deserted before the inn. The girl who had handed me the wine also went toward the village now, but she walked very slowly and looked around more than once as if she had forgotten something. At last she stopped and looked for something on the ground, but I could see that when she bent down she looked back toward me under her arm. I had learned good manners at the castle, so I approached quickly and said, "Have you lost something, lovely damsel?"

"Oh no," said she, turning red all over, "it was only a rose—want it?" I thanked her and put the rose in my buttonhole. She gave me a very friendly look and said, "Very nice playing." "Yes," I replied, "that's a gift of God." "Musicians are very scarce in these parts," the girl resumed and then stopped again, keeping her eyes cast down. "You could earn a good bit of money here—and my father plays the fiddle a little, too, and likes to hear tell about foreign parts—and my father is very rich." Then she burst into a laugh and said, "If you only didn't wag your head so while you play!"

"Dearest maiden," I rejoined, "first: don't be so formal with me; and then as to the tremolo of the head, that's the way it always is, we virtuosos are all like that."

"Oh, is that it?" returned the girl. She was about to say something more, but all at once there was a fearful racket in the inn, the door burst open with a great crash, and a thin fellow came flying out like a fired-off ramrod, whereupon the door was immediately slammed shut behind him.

At the first sound the girl had shot away like a deer and vanished in the darkness. But the figure before the door nimbly picked itself up off the ground again and now began to rail against the house with such rapidity that it was simply astonishing. "What!" he cried, "I drunk? I not pay the chalk marks on the smoky door? Wipe them off, wipe them off! Wasn't it only yesterday that I shaved you over the ladle and cut your nose so that you chewed the ladle in two? Shaving counts one mark—kitchen ladle, another mark—court plaster on the nose, another mark—how many more such scoundrelly marks do you want paid for? But all right, it's all right, I'll leave the whole village, the whole world unshaved. Run around with your beards, for all I care, till God himself on Judgment

Day doesn't know whether you're Jews or Christians! Yes, hang yourselves on your own beards, you shaggy country bears!" Here he all at once broke out into lamentable weeping and continued quite piteously in a high falsetto, "You want me to swill water like a wretched fish? Is that brotherly love? Don't you know I'm human and a practiced surgeon? Ah, I'm in such a furor today! My heart is full of compassion and philanthropy!" At these words he withdrew little by little, as everything remained silent in the house. When he perceived me, he came toward me with open arms, and I thought the madcap was going to embrace me. But I jumped to one side, and so he stumbled on farther, and for a long time I could hear him discoursing with himself through the darkness, now in a deep, now in a high voice.

In my own head thoughts a-many were circling about. The maiden who had just now given me the rose was young, beautiful, and rich—I could make my fortune here in the turning of a hand. And mutton and pork, turkeys and fat geese stuffed with apples—truly, I felt just as if I saw the hall porter coming toward me, "Take hold, tollkeeper, take hold! youthful wed eats happy bread, the lucky man gets the bride, stay at home and earn a good living." * Full of such philosophizing I sat down on a stone by the green, which was now quite deserted, for I didn't dare to knock at the door of the inn, not having any money with me. The moon shone gloriously, from the mountains came the murmur of the woods to me through the still night, and at times the dogs bayed in the village, which lay farther down the valley and was as if

* The author slyly says "good living" instead of "honest living," which is the common wording of the proverb.

buried under trees and moonlight. I surveyed the firmament, noting how single clouds slowly floated through the moonlight, and how from time to time a star fell far in the distance.

"Just this way," I thought, "the moon is also shining down on my father's mill and on the white castle of the countess. There too everything has long since been silent, the kind lady is sleeping, and the fountains and trees in the park are still murmuring as they did then, and none of them care whether I am still there or out in the world or dead." And so the world all at once seemed to me so horribly big and wide, and I so utterly alone in it, that I could have wept from the bottom of my heart.

As I was still sitting there, I suddenly heard distant hoofbeats in the forest. I held my breath and listened, and they came closer and closer, and already I could hear the horses snorting. Soon afterwards two riders actually came out from under the trees, but they stopped at the fringe of the forest and spoke furtively but very eagerly together, as I could see by their shadows, which would suddenly shoot forward across the moonlit green, and which with long, dark arms pointed now this way, now that. How often, when at home my deceased mother had told me about wild woods and warlike robbers, had I had a secret desire to experience such an affair myself. And now all at once I was catching it for my silly, sinful notions! Now I reached up the linden tree, under which I had been sitting, quite unnoticeably and as far as I could, until I had hold of the first branch, and quickly swung myself up. But I was still dangling over the branch, about to bring my legs up too, when one of the riders quickly trotted across the green behind me.

Now I shut my eyes amid the dark foliage, and did not stir or budge. "Who's there?" came a sudden call behind me.

"Nobody!" I shouted with all my might, being alarmed that he had caught me after all. But secretly I had to laugh to myself, thinking what faces the rogues would make when they turned my empty pockets inside out.

"Oho," said the robber again, "then whose are the two legs that are hanging down here?"

So there was no help for it. "All they are," I replied, "is a pair of legs belonging to a poor musician who's lost his way," and I quickly let myself down on the ground again, for I was ashamed of hanging over the branch like a broken fork.

The rider's horse shied, when I shot down so suddenly from the tree. He patted his neck and said with a laugh, "Well, we've gone astray too, and that makes us true comrades; so I think you might help us to find the way to B. It will be to your advantage." It was to no avail that I claimed complete ignorance of where B. was, and that I offered to inquire in the inn or to lead them down to the village. The fellow simply wouldn't listen to reason. He very calmly drew a pistol out of his belt, and it flashed very prettily in the moonlight. "My darling," said he to me very amiably, now wiping off the gun barrel, now testing it with his eye, "my darling, I think you will be so good as to lead the way to B."

And now I was in a very bad fix. If I hit upon the right way, then I would surely encounter the robber band and get a thrashing, since I had no money on me; and if I missed it—then I'd get a thrashing too. So I quickly made up my mind and struck into the first road that happened to lead past the inn and away from the village. The rider galloped quickly back to his companion, and the two then followed me slowly at some distance. Thus we proceeded haphazardly and really quite foolishly on through the moonlit night. The road led steadily through the forest along a mountain-side. At times one could look out over the firtops, which reached up from below and stirred darkly, far into the deep, silent valleys; here and there a night-ingale sang, and dogs barked afar off in the villages. A stream murmured continuously from the depths be-low us, and sometimes it would flash in the moonlight. And with all this the monotonous tramp of the horses and the buzzing and humming of the riders behind me, who chattered incessantly in a foreign language, and the bright moonlight and the long shadows of the tree-trunks, which flowed alternately over the two riders, so that they seemed to me now black, now bright, now tiny, then again titanic. My own thoughts got utterly tangled, as if I were in a dream and quite unable to wake up out of it. I kept striding forward sturdily. Ultimately, I thought, we must get out of the woods and out of the night.

At last, now and then, long, reddish lights shot across the sky, quite faintly, as when you breathe upon a mirror, first a lark sang high up above the silent valley. Then all at once everything grew bright in my heart at this morning salute, and all fear was gone. But the two riders stretched their limbs and looked about them in all directions, and now for the first time they seemed to be aware that we probably were not on the right road. Again they chattered a lot, and I could tell that they were talking about me, and indeed it seemed to me that the one of them be-

gan to be afraid of me, as if I might even be a feign-
ing highwayman who was leading them astray in the
forest. This amused me, for the brighter it grew all
about, the more courage I felt, especially as we were
just emerging into a lovely clearing in the forest. So
I looked quite wildly about me in all directions and
whistled a couple of times on my fingers, as rogues do
when they want to signal to each other.

"Halt!" cried one of the riders all at once, so that
I fairly started. When I turned around, they had both
dismounted and had tied their horses to a tree. But
one of them came swiftly up to me, looked me quite
fixedly in the face, and then began to laugh quite im-
moderately. I must confess that this nonsensical laughter annoyed me. But he said, "Upon my word, it's the
gardener, I mean the tollkeeper up at the castle!"

I looked at him wide-eyed, but could not recall
him, and indeed I'd have had my hands full if I had
tried to recognize all the young gentlemen who rode
in and out at the castle. But he continued, with his
everlasting laughter, "This is splendid! You're on
vacation, I see, and we're in need of a servant, so stay
with us and you'll have an endless vacation."

I was quite taken aback and finally said that I was
just making a journey to Italy.

"To Italy?" replied the stranger; "why that's just
where we are bound!"

"Well, if that's the case!" I cried, and full of joy
I drew out my fiddle and played until the birds awoke
in the woods. But the gentleman promptly seized the
other one and waltzed around on the turf with him
like mad.

Now they suddenly stood still. "By the Lord,"
cried the one, "there I see the church steeple of B!

Well, it won't take long to get down there." He drew out his watch and pressed the repeater button, shook his head, and tried it again. "No," said he, "that won't do, we'd get there too early; that might turn out badly!"

Thereupon they fetched from their saddlebags cake, roast meat, and wine bottles, spread out a handsome gay cloth on the green turf, stretched out beside it, and feasted very enjoyably, sharing everything very generously with me, which did me a lot of good, as I had not had a sensible meal for some days. "And for your information," said the one to me, " — but you don't know us?" I shook my head. "Well then, for your information: I am the painter Leonard, and that chap there—also a painter—is called Guido."

Now I took a closer look at the two painters in the early morning light. The one, Mr. Leonard, was tall, slender, and dark, with jolly and fiery eyes. The other was much younger, shorter, and more delicate, dressed in old German style, as the hall porter called it, with white collar and open throat, around which fell dark-brown curls which he often had to shake out of his pretty face. When the latter had breakfasted enough, he reached for my fiddle, which I had laid on the ground beside me, seated himself with it on a lopped branch, and plucked at the strings with his fingers. Then he sang to this strumming as clearly as a wood bird, so that it went to my very heart:

> When the rays of dawn light pale
> Gild the quiet, misty vale,
> Woods and mountains wake from quiet:
> Then all wingéd creatures fly it!
> And we men, now freed from care,

Fling our hats up in the air:
Song too through the air goes winging,
So I'll join the merry singing!

All the while the ruddy beams of the morning light were playing charmingly over his rather pale face and his black, love-smitten eyes. But I was so weary that words and tones, while he was singing thus, grew more and more blurred, until at last I fell fast asleep.

As I gradually came to again, I could still hear the two painters, as in a dream, talking beside me, and the birds singing over my head, and the morning rays shone in through my closed eyes, so that it was both dark and light within me, as when the sun shines through red silk curtains. *"Come è bello!"* * I heard someone exclaim right near me. I opened my eyes and beheld the younger painter bending over me in the sparkling morning light, so that almost all one could see was his large black eyes between the dangling curls.

I sprang up quickly, for it was already broad daylight. Mr. Leonard seemed to be irritable: he had two angry wrinkles on his forehead and hastily urged us to get started. But the other painter shook his curls out of his face and quietly trilled a song to himself as he bridled his horse, until Leonard finally burst out laughing, quickly seized a bottle that was still standing on the grass, and emptied it out into the glasses. "To a happy arrival!" he cried, and they clinked their glasses, making a pretty sound. Thereupon Leonard hurled the empty bottle high into the morning glow, so that it flashed merrily up in the air.

* Italian: "How handsome he is!"

At last they mounted their horses, and again I marched briskly alongside. Just before us lay a seemingly endless valley, into which we were now descending. What a flashing and rushing, shimmering and shouting! I felt as cool and as cheerful as if I were about to fly out from the mountain across the glorious countryside.

Chapter Four

Now GOODBYE, mill and castle and hall porter! Now we went so fast that the wind whistled about my hat. To right and left, villages, towns, and vineyards sped past, making one's eyes flicker; behind me the two painters in the coach, before me four horses with a superb postillion, and I high up on the box, where I often bounced a yard in the air.

That had come about as follows: When we arrived outside of B., along came a long, lean, morose fellow in a green pilot-cloth coat, and he made many low bows before the two painters and led us into the village. There stood a splendid coach under the tall lindens before the posthouse, with four horses hitched to it. Mr. Leonard had remarked, as we rode along, that I had outgrown my clothes. So he quickly got others out of his portmanteau, and I had to put on a brand new, handsome, long-tailed coat with a vest, which looked very elegant on me, except that everything was too long and too big and fairly dangled all around me. I also got a brand new hat, which shone in the sunlight as if it had been freshly buttered. Then the morose stranger took the two painters' horses by the bridle, the painters jumped into the coach and I onto the box, and so we were already speeding away when the postmaster peeped out of the window in his nightcap. The postillion blew lustily on his horn, and so we proceeded briskly on into Italy.

I really had a wonderful time up there, like being a bird in the air without having to do the flying myself. Nor did I have anything to do except to sit on the box day and night, and at taverns to carry food and drink out to the coach, for the painters didn't get out anywhere, and by day they drew the coach curtains as tight shut as if they feared a sunstroke. Only occasionally did Mr. Guido stick his pretty little head out of the window and carry on friendly conversations with me, and then he would make fun of Mr. Leonard, who didn't like this and always grew angry at our long discourses. A couple of times, too, I came close to having trouble with my master. One time when I began to play the fiddle up there on the box on a lovely starry night, and then later on account of my sleeping. But that really was astonishing! I surely wanted to a get a good look at Italy, and every fifteen minutes I would pull my eyes wide open. But hardly had I been gazing out at things for a little while, when the sixteen hooves in front of me got so tangled and involved, shooting back and forth and criss-cross like the threads in a piece of lace, that my eyes began to water again right away, and at last I fell into such a fearful and irresistible sleepiness that there was no help for it. Then it might be day or night, rain or sun, Tirol or Italy: I hung down over the box, now to right, now to left, now backwards, and sometimes my head even dipped downward with such violence that the hat flew off my head and away, and Mr. Guido down in the coach let out a scream.

In this fashion, I myself don't know how, I had gone half through that part of Italy that they call Lombardy, when we halted one fine evening in front of a tavern out in the country. The post horses were to be ready in the adjacent village a couple of hours later, and so the painters got out and had themselves shown to a private room, in order to rest a little and write some letters. But I was very pleased at this and betook myself forthwith into the common room, hoping for once to eat and drink in full comfort and tranquillity. Things looked pretty slovenly there. The maids went about with unkempt hair, and with untied kerchiefs hanging negligently about their yellow skins. At a round table sat the men-servants in blue blouses, eating supper, and eyeing me askance from time to time. They all wore short, thick pigtails and looked as stylish as young aristocrats. "And here you are," I thought to myself as I went on eating busily, "here you are at last in that country from which those odd folks always used to come to our pastor with mouse-traps and barometers and holy pictures. What all can't a man experience, if once he quits hearth and home!"

As I was thus eating and meditating, a little man, who had hitherto been sitting in a dark corner of the room over his glass of wine, suddenly whisked out of his nook and at me like a spider. He was quite short and humpbacked, but he had a large and repulsive head with a long Roman nose, and sparse red side-whiskers, and his powdered hair stood on end all over his head, as if a gale had blown through it. He was wearing an oldfashioned discolored coat, short plush trousers, and quite faded silk stockings. He had once been in Germany, and thought he knew German to perfection. He sat down beside me and asked me now this, now that, while he kept incessantly snuffing tobacco: "Was I the *servitore?* * When we *arrivare?*†

* Italian: "servant."   † Italian: "arrive."

Were we going to *Roma?*" But I myself didn't know all the answers, and besides I couldn't understand his wretched jargon at all. *"Parlez-vous français?"* said I to him at last in my uneasiness. He shook his big head, and that was a great relief to me, for I couldn't speak French either. But all that was of no avail. He had drawn a bead on me now, and he kept on asking and asking; the more we conversed, the less did the one understand the other, and at last we both got heated, so that at times it seemed to me that the *signor* was about to peck at me with his eagle's beak, until finally the maids, who had been listening to this Babel of tongues, had a good laugh at our expense. But I quickly laid down knife and fork and went out in front of the inn. For in this foreign country I felt just as if I and my German tongue had been sunk in the sea a thousand fathoms deep, and as if all sorts of unfamiliar vermin were writhing and rippling about me there in the solitude, and glaring and snapping at me.

Outside there was a warm summer night, just right for going serenading. From the distant vineyards one could hear an occasional vintner singing, now and then there was distant lightning, and the whole country was quivering and whispering in the moonlight. Indeed, I sometimes thought that a tall, dark shape was slipping along behind the hazels and past the front of the house, peeping through the branches, and then all at once everything was still again. Just at this moment Mr. Guido stepped out on the balcony of the inn. He did not observe me, and he played very expertly on the zither that he must have found in the house, and sang to it like a nightingale:

Noisy joys of men now rest:
Whispers earth as in her dreaming,
Wondrous with her forests teeming,
What the heart had scarce expressed;
Olden times and gentle sorrow,
Soft forebodings of the morrow
Flash like lightnings through the breast.

I don't know whether he may have sung still more, for I had stretched out on the bench in front of the door, and in my great weariness I fell fast asleep in the mild night.

A couple of hours might have passed, when a post horn awaked me, pealing lustily into my dreams for a long time before I could fully come to my senses. At last I sprang up, and found that the day was already dawning on the mountains, and the cool of morning was rippling through all my limbs. Then for the first time it came to me that by this hour we had wanted to be far away from here. "Aha," thought I, "this time it's my turn to do the waking and the laughing. How fast Mr. Guido will stick out his sleepy curly head when he hears me outside!" So I walked into the little garden next to the house and close up under the windows where my two gentlemen were staying, stretched my limbs right into the morning glow, and sang in merry temper:

When the hoopoe we hear,
Then the daybreak is near;
When the sun doffs his hood,
Sleeping tastes twice as good!

The window was open, but everything remained silent up there, and only the night wind kept blowing through the grapevines which reached up into the window. "Well, what's the meaning of all this?" I cried full of astonishment, and ran into the house and through the quiet corridors to the room. But then I felt a veritable stab of pain. For when I pulled the door open everything was empty, not a coat, not a hat, not a boot. Only the zither that Mr. Guido had played on hung on the wall, and on the table in the middle of the room lay a fine, full moneybag, to which a paper was fastened. I took it close to the window and could hardly believe my eyes, for on it was actually written in large letters: "For the tollkeeper!"

But what good was all that to me, if I couldn't find my dear and jolly gentlemen again? I thrust the bag into the deep pocket of my coat, and it plumped down as into a well, almost pulling me over backward. Then I ran out, made a great noise, and woke all the men and maids in the house. They had no idea what I wanted and thought I had gone mad. But then they were not a little surprised when they saw the empty nest upstairs. Nobody knew anything about my gentlemen. Only the one maidservant—as I managed to put together from her signs and gesticulations—had noticed that Mr. Guido, as he was singing on the balcony in the evening, all at once gave a loud cry and then quickly rushed back into the room to join the other gentleman. When she awoke once, later in the night, she heard hoofbeats outside. She peeped through the little window in her room and saw the humpbacked signor, who had talked to me so much yesterday, galloping on a white horse across country in the moonlight so fast that he kept flying into the air a yard high above the saddle, and the maid crossed herself, because it looked like a ghost riding on a three-legged horse. And now I had no idea what I should do.

Meanwhile, however, our coach had long been standing hitched up before the door, and the postillion blew his horn impatiently, until he was like to burst, for he had to be at the next station at the appointed hour, since everything had been specially ordered in advance and to the minute. Once more I ran all around the entire house, calling the painters, but nobody answered, and the people of the house flocked together and gaped at me; the postillion cursed, the horses snorted, and I, completely baffled, finally leaped into the coach, the hostler slammed the door shut behind me, the postillion cracked his whip, and so away I went out into the wide world.

Chapter Five

Now WE RODE over hill and dale without stopping, day and night. I had no time at all to sit and think, for wherever we arrived, the horses were hitched up and ready, I couldn't talk to the people, and so my gesturing did no good; often, just when I was thoroughly enjoying my dinner at some inn, the postillion would sound his horn, and I had to throw knife and fork aside and jump back into the coach. And yet I didn't really know whither and why I was supposed to travel on with such exceptional rapidity.

Otherwise it wasn't such a bad life. I laid myself down, as on a sofa, now in one corner of the coach, now in the other, and got acquainted with people and lands, and when we drove through towns, I would lean on both arms out of the window and bow my thanks at the people who politely doffed their hats before me, or I would wave to the girls at the windows like an old acquaintance, and then they would always be greatly surprised and would look after me curiously for the longest time.

But at last I got very much alarmed. I had never counted the money in the bag I had found, and everywhere I had to pay out a lot to the postmasters and innkeepers, and before I knew it the bag was empty. At first I resolved that so soon as we should ride through a lonely forest I would quickly jump out of the coach and run away. But then again I felt a reluctance to leave the handsome coach all alone, in which I might otherwise have ridden to the end of the world.

Now I was just sitting there deep in thought, not knowing which way to turn, when suddenly we left the highroad and went off to the side. I shouted out of the coach to the postillion, asking him where he was driving to. But say what I would, all the fellow would say was simply, *"Si, si, signore!"* * and he went driving on over stock and stone, so that I flew from one corner of the coach to the other.

This didn't suit me at all, for the highroad ran through a splendid landscape toward the setting sun, as it were into a sea of flashing glory. But on the side toward which we had turned there lay a desolate mountain country before us, with gray gorges in it, in which it had long since grown dark. The farther we rode, the wilder and more lonely grew the region. At last the moon came out from behind the clouds and suddenly shone so brightly in between the rocks and trees that it was positively horrible to behold. We could drive but slowly through the narrow, stony gorges, and the monotonous, everlasting rattling of the carriage re-echoed from the stony slopes and far into the silent night, as if we were riding into a monstrous tomb. Only from many waterfalls, which could not be seen, there was an incessant splashing back in the forest, and the owlets kept crying from the distance, "Come too, come too!" At the same time it seemed to me that the coachman, who as I now saw for the first time had no uniform on and was not a postillion, looked

* Italian: "Yes, yes, sir!"

52

about uneasily several times and began to drive faster, and just as I was leaning good and far out of the window, a rider suddenly emerged from the thicket, galloped obliquely across the road right in front of our horses, and promptly vanished again on the other side in the woods. I was quite perplexed, for as well as I could tell by the bright light of the moon it was the same humpbacked man on his white horse who had pecked at me with his eagle's beak back there at the inn. The coachman shook his head and burst out in loud laughter at such crazy riding, but then he quickly turned around to me, spoke a great deal and very eagerly, of which I unfortunately understood not a word, and then drove on still faster.

But I was glad, not long after that, to see a light shimmering in the distance. Little by little more and more lights appeared, and they grew steadily larger and brighter, and at last we came by some smoke-blackened huts, which clung to the rocks like swallows' nests. As the night was warm, the doors were open, and I could see the brightly lighted rooms and all sorts of ragged rabble, squatting about the hearth fires like so many shadows. But we rattled on through the silent night up a stony road which led up to a high hill. Now the entire sunken road was roofed over by tall trees and pendent shrubs, then again one could suddenly see the entire firmament and survey in the depths below the broad, silent round of mountains, woods, and valleys. On the summit of the hill stood a great, ancient castle with many turrets flooded with moonlight. "Well, God be with us!" I cried out, and inwardly I had grown quite cheerful with anticipation, wondering where they would finally land me.

Probably it took a good half hour before we finally got to the top and arrived at the castle gate. This opened into a broad, circular tower, which was already quite dilapidated at the top. The coachman cracked his whip three times, so that the echoes rang out far back in the old castle, where a swarm of daws suddenly darted in utter fright out of all the cracks and crannies, and crisscrossed through the air with a great outcry. Thereupon the coach rolled into the long, dark gateway. The horseshoes struck out sparks on the stone pavement, a great hound bayed, the carriage thundered along between the vaulted walls, and the daws kept on crying all the while—so we emerged with a fearful racket into the confined, paved courtyard.

"A curious station!" I thought to myself, as the coach now came to a standstill. Then the coach door was opened from without, and a tall old man with a small lantern looked morosely at me from under his thick eyebrows. He then took me by the arm and helped me out of the coach as he might a great lord. Outside before the main door stood an old, very ugly woman in a black smock and skirt, with a white apron and a black cap, a long tip of which hung down to her nose. She had a great bunch of keys hanging on one hip, and in the other hand she held an old-fashioned candelabrum with two lighted wax candles. As soon as she caught sight of me, she began to make deep curtseys, speaking much and asking many questions all at once. But I didn't understand a word and kept bowing and scraping before her, and I really felt quite uncanny.

Meanwhile the old man had lighted up the coach

on all sides with his lantern, and he grumbled and shook his head when he failed to find trunk or luggage anywhere. Thereupon the coachman, without asking me for a tip, drove the carriage into an old shed on one side of the court which had already been opened. But the old woman invited me very courteously, by means of all sorts of signs, to follow her. She led me with her wax candles through a long, narrow passage and then up a small flight of stone stairs. As we passed by the kitchen, a couple of young maids stuck their heads curiously out of the half-open door and stared so at me, nodding and motioning furtively to each other, as if they had never seen a man in all their lives. At last the old woman opened a door upstairs; and then at first I was completely taken aback, for it was a large, handsome, imposing room with gold ornamentation on the ceiling, and on the walls hung splendid tapestries with all sorts of figures and large flowers on them. In the center stood a table all set with roast meat, cake, salad, fruit, wine, and confections, enough to make your heart laugh for joy. Between the two windows hung an enormous mirror which reached from the floor to the ceiling.

I must say that I liked all this very well. I stretched my limbs a couple of times and like an aristocrat walked up and down the room with long strides. But then I could not resist looking at myself for once in so large a mirror. True enough, the new clothes I got from Mr. Leonard were very becoming to me, and in Italy I had acquired a certain fiery look about the eyes; but otherwise I was just the same sort of beardless youth that I had been at home, and only on my upper lip did a few downy hairs show themselves.

Meanwhile the old woman kept grinding with her toothless mouth, so that it looked exactly as if she were chewing the tip of her long nose. Then she made me sit down, stroked my chin with her skinny fingers, called me *poverino*,* while looking at me out of her red eyes so roguishly that one corner of her mouth was drawn half way up her cheek, and finally went out of the door with a deep curtsy.

But I sat down at the table, while a pretty young maid came in to wait on me. I addressed all sorts of gallant remarks to her, but she did not understand me and kept eyeing me quite oddly with side glances because I ate with such relish, for the food was delicious. When I was full and got up again, the maid took a candle from the table and led me into another room. There was a sofa, a small mirror, and a splendid bed with green silk curtains. I asked her by means of signs whether I was supposed to lie on that. She nodded "Yes," to be sure, but still it was not possible, for she stood beside me as if nailed to the floor. At last I got myself another large glass of wine from the room with the table in it and cried to her, "*Felicissima notte!*" † for that much Italian I had learned by now. But as I emptied the glass in one deep draught, she suddenly burst out in a suppressed giggle, turned as red as a beet, went into the other room, and shut the door behind her. "What is there in that to laugh at?" I thought in wonderment, "I believe all the people in Italy are crazy."

Now the only thing I was afraid of was that the postillion would begin to blow his horn again right away. I listened at the window, but everything was

* Italian: roughly "poor dear, poor child."
† Italian: "a very good night."

silent outside. "Let him blow," I thought, undressed, and laid myself in the gorgeous bed. That was exactly like floating in milk and honey! Outside the windows the old linden rustled in the courtyard, now and then a single daw would suddenly dart up from the roof—until at last, in utter contentment, I fell asleep.

Chapter Six

WHEN I awoke again, the first rays of morning sunshine were playing on the green curtains above me. I simply could not remember where I was. I seemed to be still riding in the coach, and I thought I had dreamed about a moonlit castle and about an old witch and her pale daughter.

At last I quickly jumped out of bed, dressed myself, and looked all around the room as I did so. So I observed a small Arras door which I had not seen at all before. It was ajar, and I opened it and discovered a neat little room which looked very cozy in the morning twilight. Female clothing was thrown carelessly over a chair, and in a small bed beside it lay the girl who had served me at supper. She was still sleeping quite tranquilly and had her head laid on her bare white arm, over which her black curls fell. "If she knew that the door was open!" I said to myself, and went back into my bedroom, closing and bolting the door behind me, so that the girl should not be startled and ashamed when she awoke.

Outside there was still not a sound to be heard. Only an early awakened forest birdling sat before my window on a bush that grew out of the wall, and was already singing his morning song. "No," said I, "you shall not put me to shame and be the only one to praise God so early and eagerly!" Quickly I took my fiddle, which I had laid on the little table the night before, and went out. In the castle everything was still as silent as death, and it took a long time before I found my way through the dark passages and out into the open.

When I stepped outside the castle I got into a large garden which extended half way down the hill in broad terraces, one below the other. But the gardening there was slovenly. The walks were all overgrown with tall grass, the box-tree figures had not been trimmed and stuck out long noses into the air like ghosts, or pointed caps a yard high, so that in the dim light one might have been really frightened by them. On some broken statues over a disused fountain there was even washing hung up to dry, and here and there they had planted cabbage right in the middle of the garden, and then again there would be a few common flowers, all mixed up and in disorder and overgrown with tall weeds, between which bright-colored lizards serpentined along. But looking out through the tall old trees you had a wide and solitary prospect in all directions, with one mountain top after another, as far as the eye could reach.

After I had thus strolled about this wilderness for a while in the early light, I perceived on the terrace below me a lanky, lean, pale youth in a long brown hooded coat, who was walking up and down with folded arms and long strides. He acted as if he did not see me, and soon he sat down on a stone bench, drew a book from his pocket, read very loudly, as if he were preaching, looking up to the sky at times and then propping his head in great melancholy on his right hand. I watched him for a long time, but at last I was curious to know why he was making such strange contortions, and walked swiftly up to him. He had just emitted a deep sigh, and he jumped up in fright when I came up. He was full of embarrassment, and I too, and neither of us knew what to say, and kept making bows to each other, until at last he retreated into the shrubbery with long strides. Meanwhile the sun had risen over the forest, and I jumped up on the bench and played my fiddle for sheer joy until the tones rang out far down into the quiet valleys. The old woman with the bunch of keys, who had been looking anxiously all over the castle for me to call me to breakfast, now appeared on the terrace above me and was astonished that I could play the fiddle so cleverly. The morose old man came out of the castle and joined her and was no less surprised, and finally out came the maids also, and everybody remained standing up there in great astonishment, and I went on fingering and flourished my bow more and more artfully and nimbly, and played cadenzas and variations until at last I was tired out.

But there was something very strange about that castle. Nobody was even thinking of traveling on. Nor was the castle an inn, but, as I learned from the maid, belonged to a wealthy count. Then when I would sometimes make inquiry of the old woman as to the name of the count, or where he lived, she would merely smirk, as she had done the first evening I arrived at the castle, and squint up her eyes and wink at me so slyly that I thought her not quite all there. If I drank up a whole bottle of wine on a hot day, then the maids were sure to giggle when they brought the next one, and when I even felt the desire for a pipe of tobacco and described to them by signs what I wanted, they all burst out into great and senseless laughter. Most perplexing of all to me was a nightly music which could often be heard under my window, and always on the very darkest nights. A guitar was strummed, but only from time to time, and making very soft sounds. But one time it seemed to me that from below a "Psst! psst!" was being uttered. So I quickly jumped out of bed and stuck my head out of the window. "Hallo! hey there! who's down there?" I cried. But nobody answered, and I merely heard something run off very swiftly through the bushes. The great hound in the yard gave tongue a couple of times in response to my clamor, and then all at once everything was still again, and from that time on the serenade was not heard again.

Otherwise I had such a life here that nobody in the world could wish for a better one. The good hall porter! he knew what he was saying when he told me, as he was wont to do, that in Italy the raisins just grow into your mouth. I lived in the lonely castle like an enchanted prince. Wherever I went the people all showed me great respect, although they all knew by now that I had not a penny in my pocket. I merely had to say, "Table, spread yourself!" and at once the finest foods, rice, wine, melons, Parmesan cheese, everything was there. I enjoyed it all heartily, slept in the splendid four-poster bed, went walking in the garden, made music, and helped at times with the gardening. Often too I would lie for hours in the tall grass in the garden, and the slender youth with the hooded cloak (he was a student and a relative of the old woman and happened to be here on vacation) walked around me in wide circles, murmuring things from his book, like a sorcerer, which always put me to sleep. So one day after another went by, until at last I began to grow quite melancholy from all this good food and drink. My limbs fairly began to drop out of their joints as a result of this everlasting idling, and I felt as if indolence might make me simply fall apart.

About this time on a sultry afternoon I was sitting in the top of a tall tree which stood on a side slope, rocking myself slowly on the branches over the deep and silent valley. The bees were humming about me among the leaves, but otherwise everything was as if dead to the world, not a soul was to be seen among the mountains, and far below me in the quiet woodland meadows the cows were resting in the tall grass. But from afar off came the sound of a posthorn across the wooded hilltops, now scarcely audible, now again louder and clearer. All of a sudden an old song touched my heart, one I had learned while still at home in my father's mill from a roving journeyman, and I sang:

> If far and wide you would wander,
> Then take your belovèd with you:
> The jubilant ones over yonder
> Heed not what you say or do.
>
> What know you, dark, verdant treetops,
> Of the olden days so fair?
> Ah, my homeland back of the hilltops,
> What distance from here to there!
>
> To me the bright stars are the dearest,
> They guided my footsteps of yore;
> The nightingale's song is the clearest,
> It sang by my darling's door.

The morning, Oh then joy is winging!
I mount in the silence apart
To the highest mountain-top, singing:
Bless you, Deutschland, with all my heart!

It seemed as if the posthorn were trying to ac-
company my song from the distance. While I was
singing it came closer and closer through the mountains, until at last I even heard it resounding up in the
courtyard of the castle. Quickly I jumped down from
the tree. And there was the old woman coming
toward me from the castle with an opened parcel.
"Here is something else for you, too," she said, and
handed me a dainty little note that lay in the parcel.
It bore no address, so I promptly broke the seal. But
then my whole face suddenly grew as red as a peony,
and my heart beat so violently that the old woman
perceived it, for the note was from—my lovely lady,
from whose hand I had seen many a bit of writing in
the bailiff's office. In it she wrote quite briefly, "Everything is all right again, all obstacles are removed. I
took secret advantage of this opportunity to be the
first one to write you the joyous news. Come back,
hurry back. It is so desolate here, and I can hardly
bear to live any more, now that you are gone from
us. Aurelia."

My eyes overflowed as I read this, for rapture and
fear and unspeakable joy. I felt embarrassed before
the old woman, who was again smirking horribly at
me, and I sped like an arrow into the most secluded
corner of the garden. There I flung myself down in
the grass under the hazels and read the note again,
spoke the words to myself from memory, and then
read them again, and over and over, and the sunbeams

danced through the branches and over the letters, so that they intertwined before my eyes like golden and bright green and crimson blossoms. "Is it possible that she wasn't married at all?" I thought. "Was that strange gentleman I saw her brother, perhaps, or is he dead now, or am I crazy, or—"

"All that makes no difference!" I cried at last and sprang to my feet, "for now it's clear that she loves me, yes, she loves me!"

When I once more crawled out of the shrubbery, the sun was near its setting. The sky was red, the birds were singing merrily in all the forests, the valleys were full of shimmering light, but in my heart everything was a thousand times lovelier and happier!

I shouted to them in the castle to bring my supper out into the garden. The old woman, the morose old man, the maids, they all had to come out too and seat themselves with me at the table under the tree. I drew out my fiddle and played and ate and drank by turns. Then they all grew jolly, and the old man stroked the peevish wrinkles out of his face and drained glass after glass; the old woman kept up an incessant chatter, God knows what; while the maids began to dance with each other on the greensward. At last the pale student also emerged inquisitively, cast a few scornful glances at the tumult, and was about to proceed quite haughtily on his way. But I lost no time, jumped up in a jiffy, caught him before he knew it by his long-tailed coat, and waltzed around with him lustily. Now he made an effort to dance very daintily and in the latest style, and he footed it so zealously and artfully that the sweat streamed down his face and his long coattails floated about us like a wheel. But at the same time he would sometimes look at me so oddly, rolling his eyes, that I began to be positively afraid of him and suddenly let him go again.

Now the old woman would have given anything to know what was in the letter, and why I was suddenly feeling so merry today. But that was much too long a story for me to be able to explain it all to her. I merely pointed to some cranes that were just then sailing through the air high above us, and said, "I too would now have to go away, like that, on and on and far away!"—At that she opened her withered eyes very wide and glared like a basilisk at me, now across at the old man. Then I observed how the two furtively put their heads together as often as I turned away, and talked very eagerly together, looking askance at me now and then.

I was struck by this. I kept wondering what they might be intending to do with me. This made me grow quieter, and anyway the sun had long since set, and so I wished them all a good night and went thoughtfully up into my bedroom.

Inwardly I was so happy and restless that I kept walking up and down the room for a long time. Outside the wind was rolling heavy black clouds past the big tower, and in the thick darkness one could hardly make out the nearest hilltops. Presently I thought I heard voices down below in the garden. I put out my light and stationed myself by the window. The voices seemed to come closer, but they were conversing very softly. All at once a small lantern which one of the figures was carrying under his cloak threw out a long beam. Now I could recognize the surly castle warden and the old housekeeper. The light flashed over the face of the old woman, which had never seemed so horrible to me before, and over a long knife which she was holding in her hand. At the same time I could see that they were both looking up at my window. Then the warden again wrapped himself more tightly in his cloak, and soon all was dark and still once more.

"What are they doing?" I thought, "out there in the garden at this late hour?" I shuddered, for I thought of all the murder stories I had ever heard in my life, all about witches and robbers who slaughter human beings to eat their hearts. While I was thus deep in thought, along came footsteps, first up the stairs, then down the long corridor and quite softly up to my door, while at times it seemed as if voices were secretly whispering to each other. Quickly I leaped to the other end of the room and behind a large table, which I was going to lift up before me as soon as anything stirred and thus charge toward the door with all my might. But in the darkness I over-turned a chair, making a fearful racket. Then all at once everything was quite still outside. I listened behind the table and kept staring at the door as if I were trying to pierce it with my eyes, so that they were fairly popping out of my head. When I had thus kept so still that after a time one could have heard the flies crawling up the wall, I heard somebody on the outside very softly thrust a key into the keyhole. I was just about to lunge forward with my table, but the key was slowly turned around in the lock three times, then it was cautiously withdrawn, and quiet feet shuffled down the corridor and down the stairs.

Now I drew a deep breath. "Oho," I thought, "there they have locked me in, so that they can have an easier time of it once I'm fast asleep." I promptly investigated the door. Sure enough, it was locked tight, and so was the other door behind which the pretty pale maid slept. That had never happened before, all the time I had been living in the castle.

So here I was a captive in a foreign land! The lovely lady was probably standing right now at her window and looking out across the silent park towards the highroad, to see whether I wasn't already marching along with my fiddle past the tollhouse, the clouds were scudding across the sky, time was passing—and I couldn't get away from here! Oh, I had such an ache in my heart, and I didn't know what in the world to do. And all the while, when the leaves rustled outside or a rat scuttled across the floor, I kept feeling as if the old woman had secretly entered through a hidden Arras door and was now prowling and sneaking softly through the room with her long knife.

As I sat thus on my bed full of anxious thoughts, all at once I heard again, for the first time in a great while, that nocturnal music under my window. At the first sound of the guitar I felt exactly as if a beam of morning light had suddenly flashed through my soul. I tore open the window and called down in a low voice to say that I was awake. "Psst, psst!" came the answer from below. Now I didn't hesitate long, but stowed away my fiddle and my letter, swung myself out of the window, and clambered down the cracked old wall, getting handholds on the bushes that were growing in the cracks. But some decayed bricks gave way and I began to slip, and slid down faster and faster, until at last I came down on both feet with a thud that made my brain-box rattle.

Scarcely had I thus touched ground in the garden, when somebody embraced me with such impetuosity that I shrieked. But this good friend quickly put his fingers on my mouth, seized me by the hand, and then led me out of the shrubbery into the open. Now I was astonished to recognize in him the nice, tall student, with a guitar hanging on a broad silk ribbon around his neck. I described to him now with the greatest rapidity my desire to get out of the garden. But he seemed to have known all this for a long time, and he led me by all sorts of hidden and roundabout ways to the lower gate in the garden wall. But there we were again, for it too was tightly locked! But the student had foreseen that too, and he pulled out a great key and cautiously unlocked it.

When we stepped out into the forest, and just as I was about to ask him for the best way to get to the nearest town, he suddenly plumped down before me on one knee, lifted one hand up very high, and began to curse and swear so that it was terrible to hear. I hadn't the least idea what he wanted, and I merely kept hearing *Idio* * and *cuore* † and *amore* ** and *furore!* †† When at last he even began to shuffle toward me on both knees, ever faster and nearer, I suddenly became quite horror-stricken, for I perceived that he was demented, and I ran without once looking back into the densest part of the woods.

Then I heard the student calling after me like a maniac. Soon afterward another and heavier voice gave answer from the castle. I just thought to myself that they would be looking for me. The road was unknown to me, the night was dark, and I might easily fall into their hands again. So I climbed up into

---

* Italian, from *il dio;* roughly, "my God."
† Italian: "heart."
** Italian: "love."
†† Italian: "frenzy" or "madness."

the top of a tall fir to wait for a better chance to flee.

From there I could hear how up at the castle one voice after another came to life. Some lanterns appeared and cast their wild red gleams over the ancient masonry of the castle and then away from the hill and far out into the black night. I commended my soul to the dear God, for the confused tumult grew ever louder and came closer and closer. At last the student rushed past my tree with a lighted torch so fast that his coattails floated way out behind him in the wind. Then gradually they all seemed to be turning toward another side of the hill, for the voices sounded more and more distant, and again the wind murmured through the silent forest. So then I quickly descended from my tree and ran breathlessly away, out into the valley and the night.

Chapter Seven

I HAD HURRIED along by day and night, for there was a humming in my ears for a long time, as if the people of the castle, with their shouting and their torches and long knives, were still coming after me. Meanwhile I learned that I was only a few miles away from Rome. The joy of that almost gave me a shock. For even at home as a child I had heard many wonderful tales of the splendor of Rome, and when I used to lie outside the mill in the grass on Sunday afternoons, and everything about me was so still, I would imagine Rome to be like the clouds sailing over me, with wondrous mountains and deep gorges along the blue sea, and with golden gates and tall, shining towers, from which angels sang in garments of gold. Once again it was long after nightfall, and the moon was shining in full glory, when I at last stepped out of the forest onto a hilltop and all at once saw the city in the distance before me. The sea gleamed from afar, the sky glittered and sparkled endlessly with its innumerable stars, and below it lay the holy city, of which only a long streak of mist could be detected, like a sleeping lion on the silent earth, and hills stood about like dark giants keeping watch over it.

Now I first came out upon a great and lonely heath, where it was as dim and still as the grave. Only here and there stood an old, tumble-down wall, or a withered and wondrously twisted bush; sometimes nightbirds whirred through the air, and my own shadow kept sweeping along beside me, long and dark in the solitude. They say that an ancient city and Lady Venus lie buried here, and that the old pagans still climb up out of their graves at times, to walk across the heath in silent nights and mislead the wanderer. But I kept walking straight ahead and let nothing disturb me. For the city rose up ever more clearly and splendidly before me, and the high forts and gates and golden domes shone in the bright moonlight as gloriously as if angels in garments of gold were really standing on the battlements and singing out to me through the silent night.

So at last, after passing some little houses, I walked through an ornate gateway into the celebrated city of Rome. The moon shone down between the palaces as if it were bright daylight, but all the streets were empty by now, and only here and there lay some ragged fellow as still as a corpse, sleeping on a marble threshold in the mild night. And the fountains gushed and murmured in the silent squares, and the gardens along the street interposed their whispers and filled the air with refreshing odors.

Now as I was sauntering along in this same fashion, and what with rapture, moonlight, and fragrance not knowing which way to go, a guitar became audible from far within a certain garden. "My heavens," I thought, "the mad student with the long coat must have secretly run after me!" Presently a lady in that garden began to sing with excessive sweetness. I stood just as if enchanted for it was the voice of the lovely and gracious lady, and it was the same Italian song that she had often sung by the window at home.

At that the sweet, bygone time came back to me with such vividness that I could have wept bitterly, recalling the silent garden before the castle in the early hours of morning, and how blissful I had been there behind the bush until that stupid fly got into my nose. I could restrain myself no longer. I clambered up over the grilled gate with the help of the gilded ornaments, and swung myself down into the garden from which the singing had come. Then I perceived that a slender white form was standing at some distance behind a poplar, and that at first it looked toward me with surprise when I climbed over the gate, but then all at once shot through the dark garden toward the house so fast that one could hardly see her foot it in the moonlight. "That was she herself!" I cried out, and my heart throbbed for joy, for I knew her at once by her nimble little feet. The only trouble was that in jumping down from the garden gate I had twisted my right foot a bit, and so I had to shake out my leg a couple of times before I could run after her to the house. But in the meantime they had locked and bolted doors and windows. I knocked quite meekly, listened and knocked again. Then I was certain that there was a soft whispering and giggling inside, and once it seemed to me that two bright eyes could be seen flashing between the shutters in the moonlight. Then all at once everything was still again.

"It's only that she doesn't know who it is," I thought, and I drew out the fiddle, which I always carry around with me, paced up and down on the walk before the house, and played and sang the song about the lovely lady, and for sheer pleasure I played all my songs through, all those I had played in the castle park on lovely summer nights, or on the bench out-side my little house, so that they would ring out afar, up to the windows of the castle. But it was all to no avail, there was not a step or a stir in the whole house. So at last I sadly pocketed my fiddle and laid myself down on the doorstep, for I was very weary from my long pilgrimage. The night was warm, the flower beds before the house smelled so sweet, and a fountain farther on in the garden kept splashing all the time. I dreamed of sky-blue flowers, of lovely, dark green, solitary valleys, where springs murmured and brook-lets flowed and gay-colored birds sang wondrously, until at last I fell fast asleep.

When I awoke, the morning air was stealing through all my limbs. The birds were already wakeful and were twittering in the trees around me as if they were trying to make a fool of me. Quickly I jumped up and looked about me on all sides. The fountain in the garden was still playing, but in the house there was not a sound to be heard. I peeped through the green blinds into one of the rooms. There was a sofa and big round table with a gray linen cover over it, and all the chairs were standing along the walls in perfect order and in position; but on the outside the blinds were let down at all the windows, as if the entire house had been uninhabited for many years. So I was seized with a veritable horror of the lonely house and garden and of the white figure I had seen. Without looking back at all I ran through the quiet arbors and paths and quickly climbed up the garden gate. But then I remained sitting there as if enchanted, suddenly gazing down from the high grille into the splendid city. There was the morning sun flashing and sparkling on the roofs far and wide and down into the long, silent streets, so that I had to shout aloud and leaped down full of joy into the street.

But whither should I turn in this great and alien city? Moreover, the perplexing night and the Italian song of the lovely lady that I had heard in the garden were still going around in my head. At last I seated myself on the stone fountain which stood in the middle of a deserted square, washed the sleep out of my eyes with the clear water, and sang;

> And if I were a bird,
> I know what I'd be singing,
> And had two little wings,
> I know just where I'd be winging!

"Well, merry lad, you sing like a lark at the first ray of dawn!" said a young man to me suddenly, having come up to the fountain while I was singing my song. But when I heard German spoken thus unexpectedly, it was just as if the church bell in my village were suddenly ringing in my ears on a quiet Sunday morning. "Now God bless you, worthy fellow countryman!" I cried out and leaped down from the stone fountain in great glee.

The young man smiled and looked me over from head to foot. "But what are you doing in Rome, anyway?" he asked at last. And at first I didn't know what to say, for I didn't feel like telling him that at this moment I was running after my lovely lady. "What I'm doing," I replied, "is to knock about the place a bit in order to see the world."

"Is that it!" responded the young man, laughing loudly. "Why, then our vocation is the same. That's just what I am doing, in order to see the world and then to paint it."

"So you're a painter!" I cried out gaily, for that reminded me of Mr. Leonard and Mr. Guido. But the gentleman didn't give me a chance to say anything.

"I think," he said, "you'd better go along and breakfast with me, and I'll make such a likeness of you as will be a joy to behold!" That sounded fine to me, and now I strolled with the painter through the empty streets, where only here and there a few window shutters were just being opened, and now a pair of white arms, now a sleepy little face peeped out into the fresh morning air.

He led me here and there for a long time through a great lot of twisting, narrow, and dark alleys, until we finally whisked into an old smoke-blackened house. There we mounted one dark staircase after another, as if we were going to climb up to heaven. Then we stood still under the roof in front of a certain door, and the painter began to search in all his pockets, before and behind, with great celerity. But this time he had forgotten to lock his door and had left the key in the room. For he had gone out before dawn, as he told me while we walked along, beyond the city limits, to get a look at the countryside at daybreak. He merely shook his head and pushed the door open with his foot.

That was a long, long, great room, big enough to dance in—if only the entire floor hadn't been covered with things. But there lay boots, papers, clothing, upset paint pots, in utter confusion; in the middle stood large scaffoldings such as are used for picking pears, and big pictures leaned against all the walls. On a long wooden table there was a dish, with bread and butter on it alongside a blob of paint. A bottle of wine stood hard by.

"Now first of all eat and drink, comrade!" the painter cried to me. And I was quite ready to butter a couple of slices of bread, but now there was no knife, either. First we had to rummage around for a long time in the papers on the table, before we finally found the knife under a big bundle. Thereupon the painter pulled open the window, so that the fresh morning air merrily penetrated the entire room. There was a glorious view from it, across the city and far over to the mountains, where the morning sun was gaily lighting up the white country houses and the vineyards. "Hurrah for our cool-green Germany yonder behind the mountains!" cried the painter, drinking his toast from the wine bottle, which he then handed to me. I politely drank his health, and in my heart I saluted over and over my lovely homeland there in the distance.

But meantime the painter had moved closer to the window a wooden frame to which a very large piece of paper was fastened. On the paper there was only an old hut, sketched in very skillfully with heavy black strokes. In it sat the Holy Virgin, with an excessively beautiful and joyous and yet very doleful face. At her feet lay the child Jesus in a little nest of straw, looking friendly, but with large and serious eyes. Outside on the threshold of the open hut knelt two shepherd boys with crook and bag.

"You see," said the painter, "I want to put your head on one of the shepherds, and in this fashion your face will get around in the world a bit, and if God will they shall still be taking pleasure in it when we two are long since buried and are ourselves kneeling as quietly and joyously before the Holy Mother and her son as these happy lads here." Thereupon he seized an old chair, of which however, as he attempted to pick it up, half the back came off in his hand. Quickly he fitted it together again, shoved it in front of the easel, and now I had to sit down on it and turn my face a little sidewise toward the painter. So I sat for a few minutes quite still, without budging. But I don't know how it was, at last I could not rightly stand it any more, for now I had an itching here, and now one there. Moreover, just opposite me there hung the half of a broken mirror, and I couldn't help looking into it all the time and making all sorts of faces and the like, just when he was painting, to while away the time. The painter observed this and finally burst out laughing, making a sign with his hand that I should get up again. Anyway, my face on the shepherd's body was already finished, and it looked so nice that I quite approved of myself.

Now he went on sketching industriously in the fresh cool of morning, singing a little ditty the while and at times looking out of the open window at the splendid prospect. But meanwhile I cut myself another hunk of bread and buttered it, and with this in hand I walked up and down the room and studied the pictures that were set up along the wall. Two of them I liked especially well. "Did you paint these too?" I asked the painter. "I should say not!" he replied, "those are by the famous masters Leonardo da Vinci and Guido Reni—but that's all Greek to you!"

This windup of his speech annoyed me. "O," I replied quite calmly, "I know those two masters as I do my own pocket."

Then he did open his eyes. "How so?" he asked quickly.

"Well," said I, "didn't I travel along with them by night and day, on horseback and on foot and in the coach, so that the air whistled around my hat, and didn't I lose them in the inn and then keep on traveling all by myself in their coach with special relays, so that that bombshell of a coach kept riding on two wheels over the horrible stones, and—"

"Oho! Oho!" broke in the painter, staring at me as if he thought I was crazy. But then he suddenly burst out into loud laughter. "Ah," he cried, "I begin to catch on: you traveled with two painters named Guido and Leonard?" When I confirmed that, he sprang up quickly and once more looked me over from head to foot very closely. "I do believe," he said, "actually—do you play the violin?" I thumped upon my coat pocket, so that the fiddle in it made a sound. "Well, as true as I live," responded the painter, "there was a countess here from Germany, and she had inquiries made in every corner of Rome concerning the two painters and also a young musician with a fiddle."

"A young countess from Germany?" I cried out in rapture, "did the hall porter come along too?"

"Oh well, I don't know about all that," answered the painter, "for I only saw her a few times at the house of a friend of hers, who however does not live in the city. Do you know her?" he continued, suddenly lifting a linen cover from a large picture in a corner of the room. Then I felt exactly as when the shutters of a dark room are opened and the morning sun suddenly flashes across your eyes, for it was—the sweet and lovely lady! She was standing in the garden in a black velvet dress, and lifting the veil from her face with one hand she looked quietly and pleasantly out into a wide and splendid land. The longer I looked, the more it seemed to me to be the garden by the castle, and the flowers and branches were swaying lightly in the wind, and in the depths below I thought I could see my little house and the highroad running far through the green land and the Danube and the distant blue mountains.

"It's she, it's she!" I cried at last, snatched up my hat, and dashed out of the door, and down the many flights of stairs, and merely heard the astonished painter shout after me that I should come back toward evening, and then perhaps we could find out some more.

Chapter Eight

WITH GREAT CELERITY I hurried through the city, in order to report again at once to the house where the lovely lady had sung the evening before. In the meantime everything had come to life in the streets; gentlemen and ladies were promenading in the sunshine, bowing and saluting each other right and left, superb coaches came rattling by, and from all the spires pealed the summons to mass, so that the tones rang out above the din and were mingled wondrously in the clear air. I was as if drunk with joy and with the clamor, and in my delight I kept running straight ahead, until at last I no longer had any idea where I was. It was like an enchantment, as if the quiet square with the fountain and the garden and the house had merely been a dream, and in the bright light of day it had all vanished again from the earth.

I couldn't ask anybody, for I did not know the name of the square. And at last it began to grow very sultry, the sunbeams shot down upon the pavement just like flaming arrows, the people crawled into their houses to hide, the blinds were again closed everywhere, and all at once the streets were as still as death. At last I flung myself down in utter despair before a large and handsome house, before which a pillared balcony cast a broad shadow, and viewed now the quiet city, which in this sudden solitude at the bright midday hour looked positively awesome, now the deep blue and wholly cloudless sky, until excessive weariness made me fall fast asleep. Then I dreamt that I was lying near my village on a lonely green meadow, while a warm summer rain was spraying and gleaming in the sun, which was just going down behind the mountains, and when the raindrops fell on the turf they were nothing but lovely, bright flowers, so that I was completely covered with them.

But how astonished I was when I woke up and really saw a lot of fresh pretty flowers lying on and around me! I sprang up, but could observe nothing out of the ordinary except a window clear at the top of the house above me, quite full of fragrant plants and flowers, behind which a parrot was incessantly chattering and screaming. Now I picked up the scattered flowers, tied them together, and stuck the bouquet into my buttonhole. But then I began to converse a bit with the parrot, for it amused me to see how he kept climbing up and down in his gilded cage with all sorts of queer contortions, always stepping awkwardly over his own big toe in the process. But before I knew it, he shouted *"furfante!"* * at me. Even though he was an unreasoning creature, it vexed me all the same. I scolded back at him, and at last we both got into a great temper, and the more I scolded in German, the more he gurgled back at me in Italian.

All at once I heard somebody laughing behind me. I turned around quickly. It was the painter I had met that morning. "What mad pranks are you up to now!" he said. "I've been waiting for you this half hour. The air is cooler again, so let's go to a garden outside the city, where you will find a number of

* Italian: "rascal, good-for-nothing."

fellow-countrymen and perhaps get some word of the German countess."

At this I was excessively delighted, and we set out on our walk at once, hearing the parrot scolding away behind me for the longest time.

After we had left the city, climbing for a long time up narrow, stony footpaths among country-houses and vineyards, we arrived at a small garden on a height, where several young men and maids were sitting out in the open about a round table. As soon as we came up, they all motioned to us to keep quiet, pointing toward the other side of the garden. There, in a large arbor overgrown with green, sat two pretty women at a table facing each other. One of them sang, the other played the guitar. Behind the table and between them stood a pleasant looking man who beat time now and then with a little stick. Through the vines gleamed the evening sunshine, now playing over the wine bottles and fruits with which the table was dotted, now over the full, round, dazzlingly white shoulders of the lady with the guitar. The other one seemed to be in ecstasies and sang in Italian with quite extraordinary art, so that the cords on her neck puffed out.

Now just as she was sustaining a long cadenza with eyes turned skyward, and the man beside her with the raised baton was watching for the moment when she would again take up the regular beat, and nobody in the entire garden ventured to so much as breathe, suddenly the garden gate flew wide open, and a very heated girl followed by a young man with a pale and delicate face rushed in, quarreling violently. The startled conductor stood there with his lifted wand like a sorcerer turned to stone, although the singer had long since finished her long trill with a sudden snap and risen to her feet in anger. All the rest hissed furiously at the newcomer.

"Barbarian!" cried one of those at the round table to him, "here you plunge right into the midst of the ingenious tableau of the beautiful description which the late Hoffmann, on page 347 of the 'Lady's Pocketbook for 1816,' gives of the finest picture by Hummel which was to be seen at the Berlin art exhibit in the autumn of 1814!" * But all this was of no avail. "Oh stuff!" replied the young man, "you with your tableaux of tableaux! Give me my own painting in place of all others, and my girl for me alone! That's the way I want it! O you faithless, you false one!" he then went on anew to the poor girl, "you soul of a critic, who seek in painting nothing but the glint of silver and in the poet's art only the golden thread, and who have no sweetheart but just one 'treasure' after another! I wish you hereafter, instead of an honest, picturesque dauber, some old Duca with a whole mine of diamonds on his nose, and a silver glint on his bald pate, and with gilt edges on his few remaining hairs! Come now, out with that villainous note you hid away from me a moment ago! What new thing have you been hatching out? From whom is that thing, and to whom is it?"

But the girl resisted stoutly, and the more eagerly the others surrounded the enraged young man and tried to console and comfort him with a great clamor, the more heated and madder he grew with the uproar, and especially because the girl was also unable to hold

*Eichendorff's scene follows closely that described by E. T. A. Hoffmann at the beginning of his story "The Fermata," as deriving from a painting by J. E. Hummel.

her tongue, until at last she flew in tears out of the midst of the little knot of people and all at once and quite unexpectedly flung herself on my breast to seek my protection. I put myself at once in the proper attitude but as the others in the noisy crowd were not heeding us for the moment, she suddenly turned her little face up to mine and with perfectly calm expression whispered in my ear very softly and rapidly, "You disgusting tollkeeper! It's on your account that I have to endure all this. Here, take that miserable slip and pocket it, you'll find our address written on it. So then at the appointed hour, as you enter the gate, keep always to the right along that lonely street!"

For sheer astonishment I could not get out a word, for as I now took a good look at her, all at once I recognized her: actually, it was the saucy lady's maid from the castle, who had brought me the bottle of wine on that lovely Sunday evening long ago. At no other time had she seemed to me as pretty as now, leaning up against me all flushed and hot, so that her black curls hung down over my arm. "But, revered damsel," I said in great surprise, "how do you come—"

"For heaven's sake, hush! quiet now!" she replied, quickly springing away from me and across to the other side of the garden before I had time to collect my wits.

Meanwhile the others had almost completely forgotten their first topic, but went on quarreling with each other quite amusingly, attempting to prove to the young man that he was really drunk, which (they said) was not at all seemly for an honor-loving painter. The stout and nimble man in the arbor, who—as I later learned—was a great connoisseur and lover of the arts and in the interest of science was fond of being in everything, had thrown aside his baton and eagerly made his fat face, which fairly shone with friendliness, constitute one flank in the thickest of the fray, trying to mediate and mitigate everything, while at intervals he kept repeating his regret about the long cadenza and the beautiful tableau, which he had been at great pains to assemble.

As for me, there was a starry lightness in my heart, as on that blissful Saturday evening, when I sat by the wine bottle at the open window and played on my fiddle until far into the night. As the uproar seemed likely to find no end at all, I briskly got out my violin again and played without much reflection an Italian dance that they use there in the mountains and that I had picked up at the lonely old castle on the hill.

At this they all pricked up their ears. "Bravo, bravissimo, a delightful idea!" cried the merry art-lover, running forthwith from one to the other to get up a rustic *divertissement*,* as he called it. He himself started things off by extending his hand to the lady who had played the guitar in the arbor. Thereupon he began to dance with extraordinary skill, writing all sorts of letters on the turf with his toes, executing veritable trills with his feet, and making from time to time quite passable leaps in the air. But he soon had enough of it, for he was somewhat corpulent. His leaps grew shorter and more awkward, until at last he left the circle altogether, coughing violently and incessantly wiping off the perspiration with his snow-white handkerchief. Meanwhile the young man, who had entirely recovered his common sense by now, had

* French: roughly "amusement, entertainment."

fetched castanets from the tavern, and before I knew it they were all dancing under the trees in gay confusion. The sun, now gone down, cast a few more ruddy refractions against the dark shadows and over the old masonry and the old columns back in the garden, half sunk in the earth and luxuriantly overgrown with ivy, while in the other direction, far below the vineyards, one saw the city of Rome lying there in the evening glow. There they were all dancing prettily on the green in the clear, quiet air, and my heart fairly laughed within me, as the slender maidens, and the lady's maid in the midst of them, swung themselves about amidst the foliage with uplifted arms like forest nymphs, always merrily clacking the castanets in the air as they moved. I could restrain myself no longer and sprang into the midst of them, cutting very pretty figures while I kept right on fiddling.

I might have pranced around in a circle in this wise for a considerable time, without noticing that the others had meanwhile begun to weary and were gradually vanishing from the greensward. And now somebody gave a vigorous tug at my coat-tails from behind. It was the lady's maid. "Don't be a fool," she said softly, "you're leaping just like a billy goat! Take a good look at your paper and follow me soon, for the lovely young countess is waiting." And with that she slipped out of the garden gate in the dim light and had soon disappeared between the vineyards.

My heart throbbed, and I felt most like running right after her. Fortunately, as it had already grown dark, the waiter kindled a light in the great lantern by the garden gate. I stepped close to it and quickly pulled out the slip of paper. On it was written or rather scribbled in pencil a description of the gate and the street, just as the lady's maid had told me shortly before. Then it said, "Eleven at the little gate."

Until then there were long hours to pass! Nevertheless I was intending to set forth immediately, for I no longer had rest nor peace in me; but now the painter who had brought me here came toward me.

"Did you speak to the girl?" he asked, "I don't see her around any more; that was the lady's maid of the German countess."

"Hush, hush!" I replied, "the countess is still in Rome."

"Well, all the better," said the painter, "then come and drink to her health with us!" and with that he pulled me, much as I might resist, back into the garden.

Here it had meanwhile become quite desolate and deserted. The merry guests were strolling to town, each with his sweetheart on his arm, and one could still hear them, through the quiet evening, chatting and laughing among the vineyards, growing more and more distant, until at last the voices were lost, far down in the valley, in the murmurs of the trees and the river. I was still there with my painter and Mr. Eckbrecht—that was the name of the other young painter who had been so quarrelsome—and nobody else. The moon shone splendidly through the tall dark trees into the garden, a candle flickered on the table before us in the breeze and shimmered in the abundantly spilled wine on the table-top. I had to sit down with them, and my painter chatted with me about my birthplace, my journey, and my future plans. But Mr. Eckbrecht had taken the pretty young girl from the inn, after she had put bottles on the table for us, on his lap, placed the guitar in her hands, and taught her to twang a little tune on it. She could soon make her little hands obey her, and then they sang an Italian song together, first he singing a stanza, then the girl, which had a delightful effect in the lovely, quiet evening. Then when the girl was called away again, Mr. Eckbrecht leaned back against the bench with the guitar, put his feet on a chair that stood before him, and sang all by himself many fine German and Italian songs, without paying any further attention to us. The stars shone in splendor in the clear firmament, and the whole country was as if covered with silver by the moonlight: I thought of the lovely lady and my distant homeland, and this made me forget altogether the painter beside me. At times Mr. Eckbrecht would have to tune the guitar, which always annoyed him greatly. At last he twisted and yanked at the instrument so hard that suddenly a string broke. Then he flung the guitar aside and jumped up. Only now did he observe that my painter had meanwhile laid his arm on the table and his head on that, and had gone fast asleep. He quickly flung about him a white cloak which hung on a bough near the table, but suddenly bethought himself, looked sharply a couple of times first at my painter, then at me, seated himself right in front of me on the table, without much hesitation, cleared his throat, jerked at his tie, and then began all at once to deliver a speech for my benefit.

"Beloved hearer and fellow countryman!" he said, "since the bottles are almost empty and morality is undoubtedly the first duty of the citizen, when virtues begin to ebb away, I feel myself impelled by compatriot sympathy to lay some moral reflections before your mind. One might be of the opinion, to be sure," he went in, "that you are a mere youth, although your frock coat has surely seen its best years; one might perhaps assume that a moment ago you were making strange leaps, like a satyr; indeed, some might well claim that you are actually a hobo, because here you are among the *hoes* and *bowing* the fiddle.* But I pay no heed to such superficial judgments: I go by your finely pointed nose and regard you as a vacationing genius."

I was vexed by these captious remarks, and was minded to give him the right answer. But he gave me no chance to speak.

"Now just see," he said, "how quickly you get puffed up by the slightest praise. Look into your soul, and reflect upon this dangerous vocation! We geniuses—for I am one too—care for the world as little as it cares for us; no, with our seven-league boots, which are ours almost from birth, we stride without much ado straight onward to eternity. O, most lamentable, uncomfortable, spread-legged posture, with one leg in the future, where there is nothing but morning glow and future child-faces all over it, with the other leg still in the heart of Rome on the Piazza del Popolo, where the entire century, scenting a favorable opportunity, wants to march along and fastens on to the boot, enough to pull your leg off! And all this quivering, wine-drinking, and hungering solely for undying eternity! And look at my colleague there on the bench, likewise a genius; even time proves too long for him, so what will he do with eternity? Yes, most esteemed colleague, you and I and the sun, all three of

* For this outrageous punning Eichendorff must be held responsible; he wrote, "einige möchten wohl behaupten, du seist wohl gar ein Landstreicher, weil du hier auf dem Lande bist und die Geige streichst."

us rose early today and all day long we brooded and painted, and all was beautiful—and now the sleepy night draws its furred sleeve across the world and has wiped out all the colors." He kept on talking, and with his tangled hair, and after the dancing and drinking, he looked as pale as a corpse in the moonlight.

But I had long since conceived a horror of him and his wild talk, and as he now turned completely around to face the sleeping painter, I seized the opportunity, stole around the table without his noticing it and out of the garden, and descended, alone and cheerful of heart, along the vine trellises into the broad valley, which shone in the moonlight.

In the city the clocks struck ten. Behind me through the silent night I could still hear single tones of a guitar, and sometimes the voices of the two painters, who were likewise going home now, coming to me from afar. Hence I walked just as fast as I could, to prevent them from asking me any more questions.

At the gate I turned immediately to the right and into the street, and with beating heart hurried onward between the silent houses and gardens. But how astonished I was when I suddenly came out into the square with the fountain, which I had been quite unable to find by daylight. There stood the solitary summerhouse again in its garden, in the most superb moonlight, and also the lovely lady was again singing in the garden the same Italian song as the evening before. Full of delight I first tackled the little door, then the front door, and finally ran with all my might against the great garden gate, but everything was shut and locked. Not until now did it occur to me that it had not yet struck eleven. I was vexed at the sluggishness of time, but for the sake of good manners I was unwilling to climb over the gate as I had done yesterday. So I walked up and down the lonely square for a while and at last seated myself again on the stone fountain, full of thoughts and quiet expectancy.

The stars were twinkling in the sky, and on the square all was deserted and still; with keen pleasure I listened to the singing of the lovely lady, which came to me from the garden mingled with the splashing of the fountain. Then all at once I perceived a white figure which came from the other side of the square and walked straight up to the little garden door. I looked quite sharply at it in the flickering moonlight—it was the wild painter in his white cloak. He quickly pulled out a key, unlocked the door, and before I knew it he was inside the garden.

Now from the very start I had had a particular pique against that painter because of his nonsensical speeches. But now I grew quite beside myself with rage. "That slovenly genius is no doubt drunk again," I thought; "he got the key from the lady's maid, and now he intends to steal upon the lovely lady, to betray and assault her." And so I rushed through the little open gateway into the garden.

When I entered, it was quite silent and solitary. The double doors of the garden house were open, and a milky white gleam issued from within and played on the grass and the flowers before the door. I looked in from some distance. There in a superb green chamber, which was but faintly lighted by a white lamp, lay the sweet and lovely lady on a silk couch with the guitar on her arm, not thinking in her innocence of the dangers outside.

But I had little time to watch her, for just then I observed that the white figure was approaching very cautiously from the other side, creeping behind the bushes toward the summer-house. All the while the lovely lady was singing so pitifully inside there that it pierced me to the very marrow. So I bethought myself not long, broke off a stout branch, ran with it straight at the white cloak, and cried with all my might *"Mordio!"* so that the whole garden shook.

The painter, when he saw me coming along so unexpectedly, promptly took to his heels and shrieked horribly. I shrieked still louder, he ran toward the house, I after him—and I had already almost caught him, when I got my feet tangled up in the plaguy flower pots and suddenly fell down at full length in front of the door.

"So it's you, idiot!" I heard someone say above me, "if you didn't frighten me half to death." I quickly picked myself up again, and as I was wiping the sand and dirt out of my eyes, before me stood the lady's maid, who at her last jump had dropped the white cloak from her shoulder.

"But," said I quite taken aback, "wasn't the painter here?"

"Indeed he was," she replied saucily, "or at least his cloak, which he hung about me, when I met him at the gate just now, because I was cold." During this interchange the sweet lady too had sprung up from her couch and came to the door and to us. My heart throbbed hard enough to burst. But how startled I was when I took a good look and suddenly saw instead of the sweet and lovely lady a wholly strange person!

It was a somewhat tall, corpulent, imposing lady with a proud aquiline nose and high-arched black eyebrows, of an intimidating beauty. She looked at me with her large, flashing eyes so majestically that for sheer reverence I knew not what to do. I was quite confused, made bow after bow, and at last even attempted to kiss her hand. But she quickly snatched her hand away and then spoke to the lady's maid in Italian, of which I understood nothing.

Meanwhile however the preceding outcries had aroused the entire neighborhood. Dogs barked, children screamed, and now and then one heard some male voices, which came ever closer to the garden. At that the lady looked once more at me as if she would pierce me with fiery bullets, then turned back toward the room, uttering a proud and forced laugh, and slammed the door shut in front of my nose. But the lady's maid seized me unceremoniously by the arm and dragged me toward the garden gate.

"This is another time when you've made a fool of yourself," said she venomously to me as we went along.

I too was becoming enraged. "Well, devil take it!" said I, "didn't you yourselves give me an appointment here?"

"That's just it," cried the lady's maid, "my countess was so well disposed toward you; first she throws flowers to you out of the window, and sings you arias—and this is her reward! But there's nothing to be done with you, ever; you fairly trample on your good luck."

"But," I replied, "I meant the countess from Germany, the sweet and lovely lady."

"Bah," she interrupted, "she's long since back in Germany, and your mad passion with her. And the thing for you is to run back there too! She's languishing for you anyway, and there you can play the fiddle together and gape at the moon, but don't let me lay eyes on you again!"

But now there arose a fearful tumult and clamor behind us. From the other garden men with cudgels were hurriedly climbing over the fence, others were cursing and already searching the patio, frightened faces under nightcaps peered over the hedges now here, now there in the moonlight; it was as if the devil were all at once hatching out a rabble from all the hedges and bushes.

The lady's maid didn't dilly dally. "There, there goes the thief!" she shouted out to the men, pointing to the other side of the garden. Then she quickly pushed me out through the gate and banged it to behind me.

There I stood now under God's open sky, again in the silent square, forsaken and forlorn, just as when I had arrived the day before. The fountain, which shortly before had seemed to me to shimmer so gaily in the moonlight, as if little angels were climbing up and down inside it, still went on splashing as it did then, but in the meantime all my pleasure and joy had fallen into the water—I now made a firm resolve to turn my back forever on this false Italy with its crazy painters, oranges, and lady's maids, and in the selfsame hour I marched out of the gate.

Chapter Nine

The faithful hills as sentry stand:
"Who roves at morning still and pure
From foreign parts across the moor?" —
But I survey the mountains grand
And laugh at heart for utter glee,
And cry from out the heart of me
Watchword and battle cry: Hurrah,
Hurrah for Austria!

For here I'm known by all around,
Here brook and birdling greet me soft,
And forests too wave arms aloft,
The Danube gleams from yonder ground,
St. Stephen's spire, behind the lea,
Peers o'er the hill to look for me,
And if not now, then soon: Hurrah,
Hurrah for Austria!

I was standing on a high mountain, from where one gets the first glimpse into Austria, and was still joyously swinging my hat and singing the last stanza, when all at once in the woods behind me a splendid choir of wind instruments chimed in with me. I swiftly turned around and perceived three young fellows in long blue cloaks, of whom one played the oboe, the second the clarinet, and the third, who had an old cocked hat on his head, the bugle-horn—these were suddenly playing my accompaniment, until the whole forest resounded. I, not to be outdone, promptly drew out my fiddle and played and sang along briskly. At that each looked doubtfully at the other; the bugle-horn-player was the first to let his puffed out cheeks recede again and remove his instrument; at last they all stopped playing and stared at me. I paused in surprise and looked back at them. "We thought," said the bugler finally, "because the gentleman has such a long coat on, the gentleman must be a traveling English-man, out here on foot to enjoy the beauty of nature; and so we wanted to earn a *viaticum*.* But it seems to me that the gentleman is a player himself."

"Really a tolltaker," I responded, "and have come here direct from Rome, but since I have taken in nothing for some time, I have been helping myself along with my violin."

"Doesn't bring in much nowadays!" said the bugler, who had meanwhile stepped back to the woods and with his cocked hat was fanning a small fire they had lighted there. "Now the wind instruments do a little better," he went on; "when a little company is quietly eating dinner, and we unexpectedly step into the vaulted vestibule and begin to blow, all three of us, with all our might—at once a servant comes running out with money or food, just so they can be rid of the noise. But will the gentleman not take in a collation with us?"

The fire was now flaming quite merrily in the woods, the morning was cool, we all seated ourselves in a circle on the grass, and two of the players took from the fire a small pot in which there was coffee

* Latin: (via, 'way'), roughly "traveling expenses."

with milk in it, drew bread out of their coat pockets, and dunked and drank by turns from the pot, and it tasted so good to them that it was a real pleasure to watch. But the bugler said, "I can't stand that black slop," and with that he handed me one half of a large double slice of buttered bread, and then brought out a bottle of wine. "Will the gentleman not have a drop too?" I took a good swig, but I had to remove the bottle in a hurry and screw up my entire face, for it tasted like vinegar. "Locally grown," said the bugler, "but in Italy the gentleman has ruined his German taste."

Thereupon he rummaged eagerly about in his greatcoat pocket, and finally drew out along with all sorts of junk a tattered old map, whereon the Emperor was still to be seen in full regalia, with the scepter in his right hand, the orb in his left. He carefully spread it out on the ground, the others moved up closer, and they now took counsel as to the line of march they should follow.

"The vacation will soon be at an end," said the one; "we must turn left as soon as we leave Linz, and then we can reach Prague in good season."

"Well, upon my word!" cried the bugler, "whom will you pipe to on that road? Nothing but woods and charcoal burners, no purified taste for art, no decent free lodgings."

"O rubbish!" replied the other, "I like the peasants best, for they know best where the shoe pinches, and they're not so critical if you happen to play a wrong note."

"That means you have no *point d'honneur*," * re-

* French: roughly "sense of honor, pride."

plied the bugler, "*odi profanum vulgus et arceo!* * says the Roman."

"Well, but surely there must be churches along the route," remarked the third, "and we'll drop in at the parsonages."

"Your most obedient!" said the bugler, "they give small money and big sermons, saying we should not roam about the world so uselessly, but rather apply ourselves better to the pursuit of knowledge—especially if they smell me out as a future colleague. No, no, *Clericus clericum non decimat.*† But what is all this worry about? The professors themselves are still hanging about Karlsbad,** and they won't be there to the day either."

"Ah, *distinguendum est inter et inter,*" †† replied the other, "*quod licet Jovi, non licet bovi!*" ***

But now I perceived that these were students at Prague, and I felt a veritable awe of them, especially since the Latin flowed from their lips like water. "Is the gentleman also a learned person?" inquired the bugler of me at this point. I replied with modesty that I had always felt a special desire to learn, but had had no money.

"That doesn't matter at all," cried the bugler, "we too have neither money nor wealthy patrons. But a smart fellow must know how to help himself. *Aurora musis amica,*††† or in plain words: don't waste

* Latin: "I hate and shun the vulgar mob" (which has no appreciation of real art).
† Latin: roughly, "clergymen don't take tithes from each other."
** A celebrated spa, visited for its mineral waters.
†† Latin: roughly "one must make distinctions."
*** Latin: "what is allowed Jupiter, is not allowed the ox."
††† Latin: "aurora (the dawn) is the friend of the Muses."

your time eating too much breakfast. But then when the midday chimes go from spire to spire and from hill to hill across the town, and the pupils all at once burst with a great shouting out of the dark old college building, and throng through the narrow streets in the sunshine—then we betake ourselves to Father Kitchen-master of the Capuchins and find a table all set for us, or if it isn't set, at least there is a full pot for each of us on it, and then we don't ask too many questions, but we eat and perfect ourselves at the same time in the speaking of Latin. Look you, in this fashion we keep on studying from day to day. And then when the vacation finally arrives, and the others drive or ride away to their homes, then we wander through the streets and out of the gate with our instruments under our cloaks, and the whole world lies open before us."

I don't know—as he thus told his story—it cut me to the heart to think that such learned folks should be so utterly forsaken in the world. And I also thought of myself, and of how it was really not very different with me, and the tears came to my eyes.

The bugler looked at me wide-eyed. "That's nothing," he went on, "I shouldn't care to travel so: horses and coffee and freshly made beds and nightcaps and bootjacks ordered in advance. That's just the nicest part, when we step out in the early morning, and the migratory birds sail away far above us, that we have no idea what chimney is smoking for us today, and can't foresee what special good fortune may come our way before nightfall."

"Yes," said the other, "and wherever we turn up and take out our instruments, there everybody grows jolly, and if at a noonday hour we step into a manor-house in the country, and blow a tune in the hall, then the maidservants dance together out in front of the door, and their lordships have the dining hall door opened a little, so they can hear the music better, and through that opening comes the clatter of plates and the smell of roast meat out into the midst of the joyous noise, and the young ladies at table almost twist their own necks off trying to see the players outside."

"So it is," cried out the bugler with shining eyes, "just let the others pore over their textbooks, in the meantime we are studying the great picture book which the good Lord has opened up for us in the great outdoors! Ah, believe me, we are the ones that turn out to be proper preachers; we have something to talk to the peasants about, and we can bang the pulpit with our fists so that the hayseeds down in the congregation, for sheer edification and contrition, feel their hearts ready to burst."

As they went on like this, I began to feel so merry that I too would have liked to start right in and study. I couldn't get enough of their talk, for I like to converse with learned folk, where there is some profit to be had. But there was simply no possibility of getting up a really sensible discussion. For one of the students had begun to be panicky because the vacation was so soon to be at an end. Consequently he had hastily assembled his clarinet, laid a sheet of music before him on his knee, and was practising a difficult passage from a mass in which he was to play when they got back to Prague. There he sat now, fingering and piping, and sometimes so off pitch that it would go through you like a knife and you often couldn't understand your own words.

All at once the bugler cried in his deep voice,

"Listen, I've got it," and gaily slapped the map beside him as he spoke. The other ceased his zealous blowing for a moment and looked at him in surprise. "Listen," said the bugler, "not far from Vienna there is a castle, and at the castle there is a hall porter, and that hall porter is my cousin! Beloved fellow students, that's the place for us to go; we'll pay our compliments to said cousin, and he'll certainly find a way to help us forward!"

When I heard that, I started up in a hurry. "Doesn't he play the bassoon?" I cried, "and isn't he built tall and straight, and has a large and aristocratic nose?"

The bugler nodded. But I embraced him with joy and made the cocked hat fly off his head, and now we immediately resolved to ride together on the Danube mailboat to the castle of the lovely countess.

When we got to the shore, everything was all ready for departure. The fat innkeeper, at whose place the ship had anchored for the night, stood broad and benevolent in his doorway, which he completely filled, and roared out all sorts of jests and quips in farewell, while from every window the head of some girl shot out to give a friendly nod at the boatmen, who were just carrying the last parcels on board. An elderly gentleman with a gray overcoat and a black kerchief, who was going along too, stood on the shore and spoke very eagerly with a slender young lad, dressed in long leather breeches and a snug scarlet jacket, who was sitting before him on a superb English horse. To my great surprise, it seemed to me that at times they both looked my way and spoke about me. At last the old gentleman laughed, the slender lad cracked his riding-crop and galloped away, racing the

101

larks above him, through the morning air and out into the sparkling landscape.

Meantime the students and I had pooled our resources. The boatman laughed and shook his head when the bugler paid our passage entirely in copper pieces which we had been at great pains to assemble from all our pockets. But I let out a great shout when I suddenly saw the Danube so close to me again; we quickly jumped aboard the ship, the skipper gave the signal, and so we sped downstream in the fairest morning light between mountains and meads.

The birds were caroling in the woods, from both sides the morning chimes came to us from the distant villages, and high in the air one sometimes heard the song of a lark. But on board ship a canary was trilling and twittering, so that it was a joy to hear.

This bird belonged to a pretty young girl who was a passenger too. She had the cage right beside her, and on the other side she held a dainty bundle of clothing under her arm, and so she sat there by herself quite still, looking quite contentedly now at her new traveling shoes, which peeped out under her skirt, now again down at the water before her, while the morning sun shone on her white forehead, above which she had combed and parted her hair very neatly. I could see that the students would have very much liked to start a polite conversation with her, for they kept walking past her, and then the bugler would clear his throat and adjust now his tie, now his cocked hat. But they didn't really have the courage, and the girl cast down her eyes every time they got close to her.

But they were especially embarrassed in the presence of the elderly gentleman with the gray overcoat, who was now sitting on the other side of the ship, and whom they at once took to be a clergyman. He had a breviary before him, and was reading in it, but often he would look up from his book and take in the lovely scenery, while the gilt edges and the many bright-colored devotional pictures in the book flashed superbly in the morning light. At the same time he also kept good track of what was going on about him, and soon recognized the birds by their feathers; for it was not long until he addressed one of the students in Latin, whereupon all three stepped forward, doffed their hats to him, and answered him in Latin.

In the meantime I had sat down at the very bow of the boat, cheerfully letting my legs dangle above the water, and looking, while the boat just sped along and the waves below me murmured and foamed, steadily out into the blue distance, seeing how towers and castles, one after the other, emerged from the green of the shores, grew larger and larger, and then finally vanished again behind us. "If only I had wings today!" I thought, and finally, all impatience, I drew out my beloved violin and played all my oldest pieces through, those that I had learned at home and at the castle of the lovely lady.

All at once somebody tapped me from behind on the shoulder. It was the clerical gentleman, who had meanwhile laid aside his book and had been listening to me for some time. "Well," he said to me with a laugh, "well, well, *Sir ludi magister,** what about lunch there, Mister?" Thereupon he bade me put away my fiddle in order to have a bite to eat with him, and he led me to a jolly little arbor which had been erected in the middle of the boat by the boatmen out

* Latin: roughly "master of playing."

of young birches and firs. There he had had a table placed, and I, the students, and even the young girl, had to seat ourselves round about it on casks and bundles.

Now the clerical gentleman unpacked a great joint of meat and buttered bread which had been carefully wrapped in paper, also drew out of a case several bottles of wine and a silver cup lined with gold, filled it, tasted it first, sniffed at it, tried it again, and then handed it to each of us. The students sat bolt upright on their casks and ate and drank very little out of sheer respectfulness. The girl, too, merely dipped her little mouth in the beaker, looking shyly now at me, now at the students, but the more often she looked at us, the bolder she gradually became.

Finally she told the clerical gentleman that she was leaving home for the first time to go into service, and that she was just now traveling to the castle of her new mistress. I turned red all over, for she named the castle of the sweet and lovely lady. So that is to be my future lady's maid, I thought, and looked at her with big eyes, almost feeling dizzy as I did so. "There is soon to be a grand wedding at the castle," said the clerical gentleman then.

"Yes," replied the girl, who would have liked to know more about the affair; "they say it was an old and secret love, and that the old countess had never been willing to consent to it." The clergyman merely said "hm, hm," as he filled his hunting cup to the brim and sipped at it with a thoughtful mien. But I had leaned far over the table on both arms, so as not to miss a word of the conversation. The clerical gentleman observed that.

"I may tell you," he resumed, "that the two countesses sent me out to reconnoiter and see whether the future bridegroom might be somewhere in these parts. A lady had written from Rome that he left there a long time ago." When he began talking about the lady from Rome, I grew red again. "Does your reverence know the young man?" I asked in much confusion.

"No," replied the old gentleman, "but they say he is a gay bird."

"O yes," said I hastily, "a bird that breaks loose from every cage as soon as ever he can, and that sings merrily when he is at freedom again."

"And knocks about in foreign parts," continued the gentleman calmly, "goes serenading at night and sleeps in front of house doors by day."

This vexed me sorely. "Reverend sir," I cried out quite heatedly, "there you have been falsely informed. This young man is a virtuous, slender, hopeful youth, who lived in Italy in an old castle on a grand scale, who associated with nought but countesses, famous painters, and chambermaids, who knows very well how to hang on to his money, if he only had some, who—"

"Come, come, I didn't know that you knew him so well," broke in the clergyman, and he laughed so heartily that he got quite purple in the face and the tears rolled from his eyes.

"But I did hear," spoke up the young girl again, "that the future bridegroom was a great lord and extremely rich."

"Oh dear, of course, yes! Confusion, nothing but confusion," cried the clergyman, and still could not content himself with laughing, until at last he fell into a violent fit of coughing. When he had again recovered a bit, he lifted his cup on high and cried, "Hurrah for the bridal pair!" I simply didn't know what to make of the clergyman and his queer talk, but on account of my Roman adventures I was ashamed to tell him here in the presence of everybody that I myself was the lost but happy bridegroom.

Again the cup circulated freely, the clerical gentleman conversing the while agreeably with them all, so that soon everyone became fond of him and in the end they were all talking gaily at once. The students too became more and more talkative, telling about their journeys through the mountains, until at last they even fetched their instruments and began to play merrily. The cool river air was wafted through the branches of the arbor, the evening sun was already gilding the woods and valleys which were gliding swiftly past us, while the shores re-echoed the notes of the bugle-horn. And then when the clergyman grew more and more cheerful by reason of the music, and told jolly stories from the days of his youth: how he too in vacation time had marched over hill and dale and had often been hungry and thirsty, but always happy, and how the entire life of a student was really one great holiday in between the confining, gloomy schoolroom and the serious work of an official position, then the students drank one more round and briskly struck up a song, so that the notes went far into the hills around:

> To southward now are winging
> The birdlings on their way,
> And wanderers gay are swinging
> Their hats in morning's ray.
> The students now are going,

They're marching through the gate;
Their instruments they're blowing
To play this last *valet!* *

Farewell now, hither and yonder,
O Prague, afar do we wander:
Et habeat bonam pacem,
Qui sedet post fornacem! †

Through towns at night advancing,
We see the windows shine,
Inside gay folks are dancing,
All in their garments fine.
Outside we start our blowing,
And soon, ere you could think,
Our throats are dry and glowing:
Come, host, a cooling drink!
And lo, our wish contenting,
A jug of wine presenting,
Venit ex sua domo,
Beatus ille homo! **

Now sweeps the woodland shadows
The frigid Boreas,
We're tramping o'er the meadows
Through snow and rain-wet grass;
Our mantles fly behind us,
Our shoes are cracked in two,
And so we quickly mind us
To sing this ditty through:
Beatus ille homo,

* Latin: "farewell."
† Latin: "peace to him who sits by his hearth."
** "That blessed man steps from his house."

Qui sedet in sua domo,
Et sedet post fornacem
Et habet bonam pacem! *

I, the skipper, and the girl, although none of us knew any Latin, joined in the singing of each refrain with gusto, but I shouted with more glee than any, for just then I saw from afar my little tollhouse, and soon after I also saw the castle coming up over the trees in the evening sunshine.

* "Blessed that man who sits in his house, and sits by the hearth, and has good peace."

Chapter Ten

THE SHIP grounded on the bank, we quickly jumped ashore, and now we scattered in all directions in the green, like birds when the cage is suddenly opened. The clerical gentleman took a hasty leave of us and walked with long strides toward the castle. The students, on the other hand, wandered eagerly toward a remote thicket, to beat the dust out of their cloaks, wash in the neighboring brook, and give each other a quick shave. The new lady's maid, finally, went with her canary-bird and her bundle under her arm toward the inn below the castle hill, whose mistress I had recommended to her as a nice person, there to put on one of her better dresses before presenting herself up at the castle. As for me, the lovely evening shone straight through my heart, and when they had all gone their ways, I delayed no longer, but ran at once toward the castle park.

My tollhouse, which I had to pass, was still standing on the same spot, the tall trees in the great park still rustled above it as ever, a yellowhammer, which had been wont to sing its evensong every day at sundown in the chestnut tree outside my window, was again singing away, just as if nothing had happened in the world in all this time. The window in the tollhouse was wide open, and full of joy I ran to it and stuck my head into the room. There was nobody in it, but the wall clock was still ticking quietly on, the writing desk stood by the window, and the long pipe was in the corner as before. I could not help but jump in through the window and seat myself at the desk in front of the great ledger. Now the sunshine once more came through the chestnut tree outside the window and fell in greenish gold on the figures in the open book, the bees were again humming back and forth outside the open window, and the yellowhammer in the tree outside kept singing merrily on. But all at once the door from the bedroom opened, and a tall old tolltaker, dressed in my polkadotted bathrobe, came in. He stood still in the doorway, as he perceived me so unexpectedly, quickly took the spectacles off his nose, and looked at me fiercely. I was not a little startled at this, jumped up without saying a word, and ran out of the door and away through the little garden, where I just barely escaped catching my feet in the miserable potato vines, which the old tolltaker, as I now perceived, had planted there on the advice of the hall porter instead of my flowers. I had time to hear how he rushed out of the door and hurled scolding words after me, but I was already sitting high up on the tall garden wall, looking down into the castle park with beating heart.

In the park there was a scenting and a shimmering, and a jubilating of all the little birds; the open places and the paths were empty, but the gilded treetops bowed before me in the evening breeze, as if they would bid me welcome, and to one side from the deep valley the Danube flashed up at me through the trees.

All at once I heard singing at some distance from me in the park:

Noise of men now goes to rest:
Earth but murmurs as in dreaming,
Whispers through the woodlands teeming,
What the heart had scarce confessed,
Days of old and gentle sadness,
And the awesome thrills of gladness
Flash like lightnings through the breast.

The voice and the song struck me so strangely, and yet again so familiarly, as if I had at some time or other heard it in a dream. I pondered over it for a long, long time. "That is Mr. Guido!" I cried at last full of joy, and quickly swung myself down into the garden—it was the same song that he had sung on that summer evening on the balcony of the Italian inn, where I had seen him for the last time.

He kept right on singing, while I leaped over flower beds and hedges toward the song. When I stepped out from between the last rosebushes, I suddenly stood still as if spellbound. For on the greensward near the swan lake, fully lighted up by the evening glow, sat the sweet and lovely lady on a stone bench in a splendid dress, and with a wreath of white and red roses in her black hair, with downcast eyes, playing with her riding crop on the turf while the song went on, just as she had sat in the boat, that time, when I had to sing to her the song about the lovely lady. Facing her sat another young lady, and she had her round white neck, covered with brown curls, turned toward me and was singing to her guitar, while the swans slowly circled about on the quiet lake. Now the lovely lady suddenly raised her eyes and uttered a scream upon perceiving me. The other lady turned so quickly around toward me that the curls flew into her face, and when she took a good look at me, she burst out into immoderate laughter, then sprang up from the bench and clapped her little hands three times. At that very moment a great crowd of little girls in short, snow-white dresses with green and red bows on them slipped out from between the rose-bushes, so that I could not imagine where they had all kept themselves. They held a long flower garland in their hands, quickly formed a circle about me, and danced around me, singing:

> We bring the maiden-wreath to you
> Of silken stuff and azure,
> 'Tis joy and dance we lead you to
> And blissful wedding pleasure.
> Lovely maiden-wreath of blue,
> Silken stuff and azure.

That was from the *Freischütz*.* I now recognized a few of the little singer-maids as village girls. I pinched their cheeks and would have liked to escape from the circle, but the saucy little creatures would not let me go. I had no idea what all this meant, and stood there quite dazed.

Then suddenly a young man in an elegant hunting costume stepped forward from the shrubbery. I could hardly believe my eyes — it was the jolly Mr. Leonard! The little girls now opened the circle and all at once, as if enchanted, they each stood immovably on one leg, stretching out the other behind them and at the same time holding the flower garland with both hands high above their heads. Mr. Leonard took

---

* "Der Freischütz" (The fatal marksman) is a romantic opera by Carl Maria von Weber, 1821.

the hand of the sweet and lovely lady, who was standing quite still and merely glanced over at me from time to time, led her all the way up to me, and said,

"Love—on this point all the learned are agreed—is one of the most curagious* properties of the human heart, knocking down the bastions of class and rank with a single fiery glance, for the world is too small for it and eternity too short. Indeed, it is really a poet's mantle, which every weaver of fantasies dons for once in the cold world, in order to roam away to Arcady. And the farther two parted lovers wander from each other, so much the more imposing are the curves in which the travel wind blows out the iridescent cloak behind them, so much the bolder and more surprising grows the grouping of its folds, so much the longer and longer does this robe grow in following the lovers, so that a neutral person cannot walk across country without unexpectedly treading on a couple of such trains. O most beloved tolltaker and bridegroom! Although you swept in this cloak as far as the shores of the Tiber, the tiny little hand of your present betrothed nevertheless held you fast by the extreme end of your train, and however you tugged and fiddled and clamored, yet you had to return to the quiet spell of her lovely eyes. And now then, since it has come about thus, you two dear, dear, silly people, wrap the blissful cloak about you, so that all the rest of the world may drop out of sight around you—love each other like turtledoves, and be happy!"

Mr. Leonard had hardly got done with his speech

* The word "curagious" fuses "courage" and "curious" and thus attempts to follow the German word which Eichendorff invents at this point.

when the other young lady, who had been singing the little song awhile before, came up to me, quickly placed a fresh wreath of myrtle on my head, and sang very roguishly, as she placed the wreath more firmly on my hair, while her little face was close in front of me:

> This is why you have my favor,
> This is why your head is wreathed,
> Since your fiddle and its savor
> Often joy upon me breathed.

Then she stepped back again a few paces. "Do you still recall the robbers who shook you down from the tree in the night?" she said, as she made me a curtsy and looked at me so charmingly and gaily that my heart fairly laughed within me. Thereupon, without awaiting my answer, she walked around me in a circle. "Upon my word it is still the same fellow, without a trace of anything Italian! and just look at his bulging pockets!" she suddenly cried to the sweet and lovely lady, "violin, linen, razor, portmanteau, all jumbled in together!" She turned me around and around and could not stop laughing.

The lovely lady had kept quiet all this time and was too abashed and confused even to raise her eyes. Often it seemed to me that she was secretly vexed at all this talk and jesting. At last the tears suddenly burst from her eyes, and she hid her face on the breast of the other lady. The latter looked at her first in astonishment, then embraced her with heartfelt warmth.

But I stood there quite perplexed. For the more closely I looked at the strange lady, the more clearly

I recognized her, and truly it was none other than—the young painter Mr. Guido!

I knew not at all what to say, and I was just about to ask further questions, when Mr. Leonard stepped up to her and spoke with her privately. "Doesn't he know yet?" I heard him ask. She shook her head. He bethought himself a moment. "No, no," he said at last, "he must quickly be told everything, else it will merely give rise to new chatter and confusion."

"Mr. Tolltaker," he said as he now turned to me, "we have not much time now, but do me the favor of getting rid of all your astonishments here and with speed, so that you may not hereafter, by reason of questionings, astonishment, and headshaking, stir up old affairs in the minds of people, and spread new inventions and suppositions." At these words he drew me farther into the shrubbery, while the young lady fenced in the air with the riding crop that the lovely lady had laid aside, and shook the curls thickly into her face, through which however I could see that she blushed to her very forehead. "Well then," said Mr. Leonard, "Miss Flora, who is just now trying to act as if she were hearing and knowing nothing of the entire affair, had very swiftly exchanged hearts with somebody. Meanwhile along comes another and with prologs, trumpets, and drums he presents his heart to her and wants hers in return. But her heart is already lodged with somebody and somebody's heart with her, and that somebody doesn't want his heart back and will not return hers. Everybody clamors—but I suppose you have never read a romance?" I said no. "Well, then you have helped to play one. In short: there was such a confusion in the matter of the hearts that Somebody—that's myself—finally had to intervene. In a mild summer night I swung myself on my steed, lifted the young lady as the painter Guido on a second one, and so away we went toward the south, in order to hide her in one of my isolated castles in Italy, until the outcry concerning the hearts should have subsided. En route however they came upon our traces, and from the balcony of the Italian inn, before which you made such an excellent sleeping sentry, Flora suddenly perceived our pursuers."

"Then the humpbacked Signor?"

"Was a spy. So we secretly withdrew into the woods and let you ride on alone on the prearranged schedule. This deluded not only our pursuers but also my people in the mountain castle, who were expecting the disguised Flora every minute, and who, with more zeal than sagacity, took you for the young lady. Even there at the castle it was believed that Flora was living in the rocky stronghold, and they made inquiries, they wrote to her—did you not get a little note?"

At these words I drew the slip from my pocket like a flash.

"So this letter?"

"Is to me," said Miss Flora, who had hitherto not seemed to be heeding our conversation, quickly snatched the note out of my hand, skimmed it, and thrust it in her bosom.

"And now," said Mr. Leonard, "we must quickly enter the castle, for everybody is waiting for us. And so in conclusion, as is of course obvious and becoming to a well-trained romance: discovery, repentance, reconciliation, we are all once more gaily united, and the wedding is day after tomorrow!"

While he was speaking thus, suddenly there arose in the shrubbery a furious din of drums and trumpets, horns, and trombones; cannon were fired, hurrahs were shouted, the little girls danced all over again, and from all the shrubs emerged one head after another, as if they were growing out of the ground. In all this racket and riot I leaped a yard high from one side to the other, but as it was already growing dark, it was only little by little that I again recognized the old faces. The old gardener was beating the drums, the Prague students in their cloaks were playing along with the others, and beside them the hall porter was fingering his bassoon like mad. When I perceived him so unexpectedly, I at once ran up to him and embraced him vehemently. This caused him to lose his place completely. "Now upon my word, and even if he travels clear to the end of the world, he is and will always be a fool!" he cried out to the students, and went on playing, quite furious.

Meanwhile the sweet and lovely lady had secretly run away from the tumult, flying like a frightened deer across the green and farther into the park. I saw that just in time and ran after her at top speed. The players in their zeal failed to notice it, and afterward they said they thought we had started out for the castle, and so the entire crowd likewise set out for that goal with music and a great uproar.

But we had come almost at the same time to a summer arbor which stood on a sloping part of the park, with its window open toward the broad and deep valley. The sun had long since set behind the mountains, and there was nothing left but a reddish haze shimmering above the warm evening with its dying noises, out of which the murmur of the Danube came up more and more audibly, the quieter it grew round about. I did not take my eyes from the lovely

117

countess, who stood before me all heated from running and so close that I could fairly hear how her heart was beating. But now, all at once thus alone with her, I had no idea what to say, for I was overcome with respectfulness. At last I took heart, grasped her little white hand—then she quickly drew me to her and fell upon my neck, and I embraced her tightly with both arms.

But she quickly freed herself again and leaned on the window in great confusion, in order to cool her cheeks in the evening air. "Oh," I cried, "my heart is ready to burst, but I still can't realize all this, and everything still seems to me like a dream!"

"To me too," said the lovely lady. "When I came back from Rome last summer," she added after a while, "with the countess, and we had been fortunate in finding Miss Flora and bringing her back with us, but heard nothing of you either there or here—then I didn't suppose that everything would still turn out like this! Only this noon the jockey, that good and quick little chap, came galloping breathlessly to the castle and brought the news that you were coming with the mailboat." Then she laughed quietly to herself. "Do you remember," she said, "how you saw me for the last time on that balcony? that was just such a night as this, such a quiet evening, with music in the garden."

"Now who died, I'd like to know," I asked hastily.

"What do you mean?" said the lovely lady, looking at me in surprise.

"Why, the husband of your ladyship," I replied, "who stood there on the balcony with you."

She grew quite red. "What strange notions you

have in your head!" she cried out, "that was the son of the countess, just returning from his travels; and it just happened to be my birthday, so he led me out on the balcony with him, so that they might shout for me too. But I suppose that is why you ran away then?"

"Good Lord, why of course!" I cried out, and slapped my forehead with my hand. But she shook her little head and laughed very heartily.

I felt so happy, having her chat beside me so gaily and familiarly, that I could have listened to her all night. I was so utterly contented, and I fetched out of my pocket a handful of almonds which I had brought with me from Italy. She took some too, and we cracked them and looked contentedly out over the quiet land. "Do you see," she said again after a time, "that little white chateau shining over there in the moonlight? That's a present to us from the count, together with the garden and the vineyards, and that's where we are to live. He knew long ago that we love each other, and he is very well disposed to you, for had he not had you along, when he carried off the young lady from the boarding school, then the two of them would have been caught before they had had time to become reconciled with the old countess, and everything would have turned out differently."

"Dear me, sweetest and loveliest countess," I cried out, "I simply don't know where my head is with all these unexpected revelations; you mean to say that Mr. Leonard—?"

"Yes, yes," she broke in, "so he called himself down in Italy; he owns those estates over there, and now he is going to marry our countess's daughter, lovely Flora. But why do you call me Countess?" I looked at her wide-eyed. "I'm not a countess at all," she continued, "our kind Countess merely took me into her castle when my uncle, the hall porter, brought me here with him as a tiny baby and a poor orphan."

At that I felt exactly as if a stone had fallen from my heart! "God bless the hall porter," I responded in great delight, "for being our uncle! I have always thought a lot of him."

"He means well by you, too," she replied, "and always says, if only you would try to look a little more distinguished. And you must dress more elegantly, too."

"O," I cried with joy, "English frock coat, straw hat, knickerbockers, and spurs! and right after the ceremony we'll travel off to Italy, to Rome, where they have the loveliest fountains, and we'll take the students of Prague along, and the hall porter!"

She smiled quietly and looked at me with real pleasure and affection, and from the distance we kept hearing the sounds of the music, and Roman candles shot up from the castle through the silent night across the gardens, and between times the murmur of the Danube came up to us—and all was right with the world!

THE END